DUPLIN COUNTY
North Carolina

Court of Pleas & Quarter Sessions

1784-1787

(Volume #1)

Abstracted & Compiled by:
Leora H. McEachern

Copyright 1978
By: Leora H. Eachern

Copyright Transferred 1986
To: Southern Historical Press, Inc.

All rights reserved. No part of this publication may be reproduced, stored in a retrieval system, transmitted in any form, posted on to the web in any form or by any means without the prior written permission of the publisher.

Please direct all correspondence and orders to:

www.southernhistoricalpress.com
or
**SOUTHERN HISTORICAL PRESS, Inc.
PO BOX 1267
Greenville, SC 29601**
southernhistoricalpress@gmail.com

ISBN #0-89308-808-0

Printed in the United States of America

DUPLIN COUNTY COURT MINUTES

18 October 1784

"At a meeting of a County Court of pleas & Quarter Sessions begun and held for the County of Duplin at the Cross Rhodes thereof, at James James Plantation where he now lives, on Monday the 18 October, 1784, it being the third Monday of said month."

Justices present: Worshipfull Wm. Houston, Sr., Col. James Kenan & Col. Tho. Routledge, Esquires.

Ordered Plunket Ballard as State Attorney for Duplin for this Court.

Deed: Elijah Bowen to Samuel Sowell for 100 acres, proved by Shaderick Sowell; Ordered registered.

Deed: James Taylor to Absolam Langston for 160 acres, proved by Lewis Hines; Ordered registered.

Will of Phillip Rous, dec'd, proved by Ephraim Garrison & Adonijah Garrison.

Deed: Absolam Langston to William Wilkins for 160 acres, proved by Lewis Hines; Ordered registered.

Deed: Absolam Langston to William Wilkins for 200 acres, proved by Lewis Hines; Ordered registered.

TUESDAY MORNING, Court met at 9 o'clock according to adjournment.

Present: Worshipfull William Houston, Sr., Col. Tho. Routledge, Joseph Dickson, Col. Jas. Kenan & Sam'l Houston, Esquires.

Ordered Thos. Quinn overseer of road in room of Isaac Thomas & have same hands.

Ordered Arthur Bizzell Constable in room of James Bizzell.

WEDNESDAY MORNING, Court met at 10 o'clock according to adjournment.

Present: Worshipfull William Houston, Sr., Thomas Routledge, Samuel Houston & Robert Dickson, Esquires.

Deed: Jonathan Taylor to Benjamin Herring for 200 acres, proved by Daniel Herring; Ordered registered.

Deed: Hincock Hatcher to Daniel Hicks for 50 acres, acknowledged; Ordered registered.

Deed: Elizabeth Elliot to James Wright for 320 acres, proved by John Newton; Ordered registered.

Ordered James Gillispie, William McGowen, Watson Burton, Isaac Hunter, James Pearsall, James McIntire, William Stokes, Nich's Hunter, Arthur Stokes, James James, James Midleton, William Best & Edward Pearsall be a jury to lay off said road & report to next Court.

Ordered William Magee, Constable, to convene & Tho. Routledge to qualify said jury.

Ordered Capt. Thomas Quin constable in District of Capt. Hubbard's Company.

Betsey Moore & Maurice Moore, orphans of John Moore, dec'd, chose Patrick Newton as their guardian; he gave bond of £500.

Ordered Joseph Tho. Rhodes take into his possession the Estate of Benjamin Smith, late of this County, dec'd, & render inventory to next Court & that he rent out the Plantation for one year.

THURSDAY MORNING, Court met at 9 o'clock according to adjournment.

Present: Worshipfull Thomas Routledge, James Lockhart, Joseph Dickson, James Gillispie, Joseph Tho. Rhodes, Esquires.

Charles Ward, John Molten & Theophilus Williams, a committee to divide the Estate of Herald Blackmore, dec'd, reported that to William Kenan went 20 Negroes: Liddia, Sarah, Sampson, George, Diana, Sally, Hannah, Edinburgh, Venus, Jimmy, George, Doll, Cesar, Phillis, Springhall, Sampson, Will, Violet, Andrew & Charles; to Edward Blackmore, son of said Herald, dec'd, went 20 Negroes: Jude, Cork, Doll, Priamus, Abbey, Tom, Satira, Neptune, Lucy, Ned, Penny, Charles, Peter, Chaney, Ponto, Pamelia, Aaron, Quash, Castilla & Affey; Court concurred; Ordered recorded & filed.

Ordered Andrew Thally overseer of road & river in room of Daniel Teachey.

Ordered Frederick Bearfield overseer of road in room of Lutson Stroud.

Ordered tax of one shilling levied on each taxable person & four pence on every 100 acres for discharging the County contingencies for 1784.

Inventory of Estate of Stephen Cade, dec'd, exhibited; Ordered filed.

Ordered Moses Manning overseer in room of Drury Hall.

Deed: Solomon Carter to Davie Carter for 200 acres, proved by Hezekiah Blizzard; Ordered registered.

Deed: Andrew Adams to Solomon Carter for 200 acres, proved by Hezekiah Blizzard; Ordered registered.

Deed: Isaac Davison to Solomon Carter for 100 acres, proved by Hezekiah Blizzard; Ordered registered.

Bill of Sale: John Magee & Ebenezer Garrison to Jacob Williams for 3 Negro slaves, proved by William Farrior; Ordered registered.

FRIDAY MORNING. Court met at 9 o'clock according to adjournment.

Present: Worshipfull Thomas Routledge, Joseph Dickson, Thomas James, Esquires.

Appointed the following Justices to take the list of Taxables for the present year:
For Capt. Dicksons Company - James Gillispie, Esq.
For Capt. Teacheys Company - Daniel Teachy, Esq.
For Capt. Stallings Company - Thomas James, Esq.
For Capt. Kenans Company - Thomas Hooks, Esq.
For Capt. Bowdens Company - Theo. Williams, Esq.
For Capt. Barfields Company - Frederick Barfield, Esq.
For Capt. Housmans Company - James Outlaw, Esq.
For Capt. Houstons Company - Sam'l Houston, Esq.
For Capt. Fountains Company - John Farrior, Esq.
For Capt. Millers Company - Charles Ward, Esq.

Allowed William Magee 16 shillings as Constable 2 days this Term.

Allowed Owen O'Daniel 24 shillings as Constable 3 days this Term.

Allowed Isaac Millard 32 shillings for attending 4 days this Term.

William Wilkinson, Jr. issued licence to keep a Tavern or Ordinary where he now lives, near the Court House; securities approved.

Ordered the following as Jurymen for the next Court on the 3rd Monday of July next: James Midleton,Sr., William Rigby, James Dickson, James Evin, Isaac Midleton, Edward Armstrong, Charles James, Thomas Heath, John Carr, Timothy Teachy, Jesse George, David Williams, Thomas Crumpton, David Sloan, Peter Carleton, Thomas Hill, Thomas Wright, Daniel Hicks, William Ward, Lavin Watkins, George Kornegay,Jr.,Adam Reeves, John Beck, John Kitley, Silas Carter, Samuel Bowden, Richard Bradley, Jonathan Kitley, Jacob Glisson, Lewis Pipkin, Samuel Alberson, John Matchet, Joseph Grimes, John Neale,Jr., Ivey Smith, Joseph Johnston, William Hall, Robert T[?], Frederick Smith, William Burton, James Picket, Jr., Ben Lanier, Jr., Jesse Brown.

Inventory of Estate of Sarah Matchet,dec'd, exhibited; Ordered filed.

Ordered James Pearsall & William Matchet, Executors of will of Sarah Matchet,dec'd, to sell enough of perishable estate to discharge debts of said estate & make return to next Court.

Thomas James recorded his mark: crop in right ear & a half moon under left.

Ordered Thomas James, Aaron Williams, Edward Dickson, William Merrit, Jacob Matthews, Arthur Stokes, John Carr, James Mills, John Armstrong, William Rigby, Alex'r Dickson, Richard Williams, Isaac Thomas, John Farrier, William Wallace, Drury Hall, David Cannon, Jr., William Hooks, Thomas Hill, Richard Mears, William Newton, John Neale, John Chambers, Joseph Smith, Samuel Rogers, John Houseman, John Glisson, Jacob Rhodes, Lot Gregory, William Nethercut, James Bizzell, John Shuffield be summoned as jurymen for next Court.

Ordered Richard Clinton, Sampson Co., & the Executors of Edmund Mathis, dec'd, render account of estate of William Ganey, dec'd, at next Court.

Ordered William Southerland, William Best & William Kenan be a Committee to settle estate of William Pearse, dec'd, between Joseph Grimes, Administrator, & the Orphans of said dec'd & report to next Court.

Ordered [blank] in South Carolina take Deposition of John M.Muldrough in suit of Alexander Dickson against Thomas Wiggins.

Ordered [blank] in Georgia take Deposition of Robert Williams in suit of Thomas Picket against Alexander Dickson.

Ordered Robert Dickson, Hugh McCann & James Maxwell be a
committee to divide the estate of Joseph Carr, dec'd,
& to divide the estate of Barbara Carr, dec'd.

Ordered Michael Glisson overseer of road in room of James
Outlaw.

As the Jury appointed last Term to lay off a new road from
James Outlaws bridge on the NorthEast to Grove Bridge at
Thomas Routledge has not convened nor laid off said road.
Ordered Thomas Routledge, James Gillespie, James Midleton, Sr.,
Isaac Hunter, William McGowan, James McIntire, John Williams
(Burncoat), Edward Pearsall, William Best, William Frederick,
James Pearsall, William Dickson, Joseph Dickson, Thomas Hooks,
Sam'l Ward, William Hall, Robert Southerland, Nicholas Hunter
& James Midleton, Jr., they or any 12 of them, to lay off
road, crossing Goshen Swamp at the best place, & report to
next Court.

James Gillispie, Kader Bryan, Joseph Tho Rhodes, James Outlaw
& Daniel Teachey, who were commissioned Justices of the Peace
Nov. 26, 1784, qualified & took seats upon the Bench.

Presented petition of persons living on both sides of Goshen
Swamp asking to have Swamp opened & cleared for boats;
Court Ordered William Taylor, Thomas Hooks, John Beck, Lewis
Thomas, George Miller, Joseph Grimes, Daniel Herring, Thomas
Gray & William Dickson be a Committee to inspect the run of
Goshen from the mouth to Hursts Bridge & report to next Court
as to practicability of such a design.

Orson Moore, orphan of John Moore, dec'd, chose John Houseman
as Guardian; Houseman gave bond of £150.

Ordered Patiance Cade, Adm'x of Stephen Cade, dec'd, to
sell said estate & report to next Court.

Presented petition of inhabitants of Bear Swamp & the neighborhood asking for a Public Road to be laid off from the road
near the head of Bear Swamp & leading near Lewis Thomas
Plantation on the Nahunga towards the place where the Court
House now is & to join the Grove Road between the Grove
Swamp & Nahunga; Petition granted.

Ordered Lewis Thomas, William Kenan, James Kenan, Abraham
Molten, John Molten, Theophilus Williams, William Guy, James
Wright, William Newton, Felix Frederick, John Ward, Cullen
Connerly, Luke Ward, Jr., William Boyd, Thomas Hill, Robert
Wilkinson, Sam'l Guy & Luke Ward, Sr., or any 12 of them, a
Jury to lay off said road.

Ordered John Beck qualify & William Moore, Constable, convene
said Jury.

Benjamin Lanier, charged with begeting a Bastard Child of Mary Matthews, gave bond of £200.

Presented petition of inhabitants of Grove Swamp asking to have a road laid off from the Court House lot at James Pearsalls to join the Limestone road where most convenient; Granted.

Ordered William Magee, Constable, to convene said Jury [no names listed] at the house of [torn] Routledge & that [torn] Houseton qualify same.

Inventory of estate of Elix[torn] Hamilton, dec'd, presented; Ordered filed.

Inventory of estate of Phil[torn], dec'd, presented; Ordered filed.

List of sales of estate of Philip Rouse, dec'd, presented; Ordered filed.

Exhibited will of Thankful Hicks, proved by Joseph Thomas Rhodes; Ordered filed.

William Carr, Adm'r of Barbara Carr, dec'd, offers as securities Joseph Dickson & James Pe[torn], gave bond of £100.

Deed: Thomas Taylor to Elisha Jones for 345 acres, proved by James Goodman; Ordered registered.

Deed: William Hurst to William Burnam for 2 pieces of land, acknowledged; Ordered registered.

Deed: Samuel Sowell to John [torn] for 100 acres, acknowledged; Ordered registered.

Deed: Thomas Wiggins to [Nat]haniel Kinnard for 40 acres, proved by John Beck; Ordered registered.

Deed: James Williams & [torn] Williams, his wife, to James Gillespie, acknowledged; Ordered registered.

Deed: Alexander Laine to William Kenan for 430 acres, proved by Thomas Hill; Ordered registered.

Deed: James Kenan to Andrew Thally for 640 acres, acknowledged; Ordered registered.

Deed: Sutton Byrd to Lewis Thomas for 210 acres, with a Plan of Resurvey, proved by David Midleton; Ordered registered.

Deed: Charles Merrit to Benjamin Ezel for 100 acres, proved by Arthur Mathis; Ordered registered.

Deed: Timothy Murphy to James Pearsall for 2 pieces of land, proved by James Lockhart; Ordered registered.

Lease: Margaret New to John Hill for 200 acres, proved by Edward Harris; Ordered registered.

Deed: James Pearsall, Sheriff, to Thomas Hooks for 125 acres, acknowledged; Ordered registered.

Appointed Charles Ward, John Molton & Theophilus Williams a committee to settle & divide the estate of Herald Blackmore, dec'd, agreeable to will of said dec'd & report to next Court.

Grand Jury sworn: William Best, foreman, Lewis Barnes, Henry Houston, William Carr, James Dickson, JoabPadgett, James Ward, William Beck, Alexander Porter, John Boney, John Matchet, Alex'r Graddy, William Hurst, Sam'l Sowell & James Midleton.

Ordered Thomas Carelton, Constable, to attend Grand Jury.

Ordered Philip Hall, Guardian of Patiance Hall, sell perishable part of said orphans estate & report to next Court.

Patiance Cade, widow od Stephen Cade, dec'd, offered as securities Daniel Glisson & Samuel Ward, gave bond of £200 & took oath of admin'r.

Patiance Cade, admin'r, returned inventory of estate of Stephen Cade, dec'd.

John Williams took oath for qualification of Public Offices & of an Attorney to practice law in the County Courts of the State.

Theophilus Williams, security for Elisha Carrol in the suit of Thomas Gray against Elisha Carrol, surrendered said Carrol to the Court; Sheriff ordered to take him into custody, Williams discharged.

WEDNESDAY MORNING, Court met at 9 o'clock according to adjournment.

Present: Worshipfull Thomas Routledge, James Kenan, James Lockhart, Joseph Dickson, Charles Ward, Samuel Houston & John Beck, Esquires.

Rachel Hagan took oath as Admin'r of estate of James Green, dec'd; offered as securities Henry Holland & John Odom; gave bond of £200.

Appointed William Dickson, James Kenan & Lavin Watkins a committee to settle & divide the estate of John Moore agreeable to the will & report to next Court.

Deed: Joseph Winfield to Benjamin Coxwell for 150 acres, proved by Samuel Rhoades; Ordered registered.

Deed: Theophilus Williams to Rawley Mills for 50 acres, acknowledged; Ordered registered.

Deed: James Rawlings to John Blanton for [blank] acres, proved by Elijah Bowen; Ordered registered.

Deed: Clifton Bowen to John Blanton for 100 acres, proved by Elijah Bowen; Ordered registered.

Appointed Henry Faison admin'r of estate of James Faison, dec'd; he with John Fort & William Beck gave bond of £800.

Deed: John Sullivant to Stephen Gufford for 200 acres, acknowledged; Ordered registered.

Deed: Richard Parker to Henry Picket for 25 acres, proved by James Lockheart; Ordered registered.

Deed: John Halso to James Ellissa for 100 acres, acknowledged; Ordered registered.

Deed: Nicholas Briant to Andrew Wallis for 58 acres, proved by Joseph Cox; Ordered registered.

Deed: John Sullivan to James Herring for 300 acres, acknowledged; Ordered registered.

Deed: Theophilus Williams, Sheriff, to John Sullivan for 200 acres, acknowledged; Ordered registered.

Deed: William Sullivan to John Sullivan, Jr. for 400 acres, acknowledged; Ordered registered.

Deed: Alexander Armstrong to James Heath for 460 acres, proved by Joseph Dickson; Ordered registered.

Deed: James Lockheart to Nicholas Hunter for 612 acres, acknowledged; Ordered registered.

Deed: John Beck to Thomas Gray for 650 acres, proved by Samuel Slocumb; Ordered registered.

William Flowers, security for Solomon Beesley, delivered him to Court; Beesley offers as security for appearance at next Court Samuel Ward.

~~Ordered William Hall, Daniel Southerland & Gus Williams fined $5 for being absent as Jurymen.~~

Nathan Godwin, security for Joseph Davidson, delivered Davidson to Court; Davidson ordered into custody, gave John Easom as security.

Daniel Parker paid 6 pence for costs & damages which Edward C.Dibrule obtained against him.

Ordered a Commission issued Joseph Dickson to take deposition of James Evans & Elizabeth Mary Rouse on behalf of Rebecca Briant against Adonijah Garrison.

Joseph Johnson, as garnishe, confessed he had £113 in his hands of estate of Henry Eustice McCulloch.

John Johnston,Jr. issued letters of admin'n on estate of Elizabeth Hambleton, dec'd, & gave as securities Robert Dickson & John Matchet.

THURSDAY MORNING, Court met at 10 o'clock according to adjournment.

Present: Worshipfull William Houston,Sr., Thomas Routledge, James Kenan, Joseph Dickson & Robert Dickson, Esquires.

Granted Thomas Gray licence to keep a Public House on the Plantation where William Hurst now lives, on Goshen near the Bridge; offered as securities William Dickson & John Wright, gave bond.

Granted Arthur Stokes admin'n of will of Philip Rouse, dec'd, & he gave as securities James Pearsall & William Hall; gave bond of £300.

Martin Rouse, Orphan, chose as his Guardian Thomas Routledge, who offered as securities James James & Edward Pearsall; gave bond of £200.

Appointed Daniel Glisson, John Wright,Jr. & William Ward searchers for Capt. Michael T.Kenans District.

George Lassiter offered as securities Samuel Ward & Hardy Reeves for prosecution of an appeal in suit brought against him by Admin'ors of Andrew Killit, dec'd; Approved.

Arthur Stokes qualified as admin'r of estate of Philip Rouse, dec'd; Ordered to sell perishables.

Granted Watson Burton licence to keep a Public House on the Plantation where he now lives; gave as securities William Best & Jeremiah Pearsall.

Appointed Thomas Gray, Nathaniel Kinard, Thomas Flow[torn], John Haines, William Hurst, William Walk[torn], Joseph Wade, John Bradley, William Gully, Thomas Wiggins, James Oates, William Burnam, Jacob Taylor, Shaderick Davis [?] a committee to view ground from Kinnards on the north side of Goshen Swamp to William Hursts on Goshen & report to next Court on convensency of laying off a Public Road.

Ordered Arthur Stoakes, Admin'r of Philip Rouse, dec'd, to sell perishables.

Appointed Daniel Glisson collector of Capt. Bowdens & Capt. Kenans Districts; Glisson offered as securities Theophilus Williams, William Kenan & Samuel Ward.

Appointed Frederick Bearfield collector of Capt. Whiteheads, Capt. Hubbards & Capt. Millers Companies; he offered as securities Samuel Ward, Theo's Williams & William Taylor.

Appointed Nicholas Routledge collector for Districts of Capt. Gillispie, Capt. Waller & Capt. Stallins Companies; he offered as securities Thomas Routledge, George Williams & Edward Pearsall.

Archibald Carr delivered Samuel Williams & Robert Williams to Court; they offered as security James Williams, Sr. for their appearance at next Court.

Ordered Henry Houston, Loftis Worley, James Middleton (Long), William Best, William Carr, James Dickson, Charles Brown, Stephen Miller, John Matchet, Jacob Padget, James Ward, James Winders, David Cannon, Daniel Glisson, William Beck, Jesse George, Alexander Porter, Andrew Thalley, Frederick Williams, Nothial McCann, John Boney, Jacob Brown, William Southerland, John Johnson, Alexander Graddy, Samuel Sowell, James Oates, Shad'k Daniel, William Hurst be summoned as Jurymen for ensuing Court.

Ordered [?] & [?] two Negroes be added to [?] road to work under Thomas Quin, Overseer, & that John Waller, Nathaniel Waller, Stephen Williams & Francis Whaley be added to New River Road to work under Laban Williams, Overseer.

Deed: Abraham Glisson to Edward Dickson for 190 acres, proved by Kadar Briant; Ordered registered.

Bill of Sale: Philip Rouse to Elizabeth Mary Rouse, his wife, for sundry articles, proved by William Best & James Evans; Ordered filed & copy to said Elizabeth Mary Rouse.

Lewis Hedgeman & Robert Sloan offered themselves as securities for maintainance of a Bastard Child named Charlotte Brinson, begotten on Vialator Brinson by George Hedgeman; gave bond of £50.

Appointed Joseph Dickson, John Molten & James Middleton,Sr. a Committee to adjust estate of William Williams, dec'd, between James Williams, Sr., the admin'r, & Mary Williams, orphan of said dec'd & report to next Court.

Ordered Samuel Williams & Robert Williams, summoned as garnishee, attend said Committee & render account of property that may be in their hands belonging to estate of said dec'd.

Appointed Joseph Dickson guardian to Mary Williams, orphan of William Williams,dec'd; Ordered James Williams, Sr., admin'r, deliver all monies, notes, bonds & other accounts & papers belonging to said estate to Joseph Dickson, he to give bond of £100.

Deed: Samuel Ward to Rubin Johnston for 100 acres, acknowledged; Ordered registered.

Deed: David Cannon to Kadar Bryan for 200 acres, proved by Samuel Williams; Ordered registered.

Deed: Dennis Cannon to Kadar Bryan for 200 acres, proved by Robert Williams; Ordered registered.

Deed: Daniel Herring to Stephen Herring for 3 acres, acknowledged; Ordered registered.

Deed: Theophilus Williams to Kilby Faison for 400 acres, proved by Michael T.Kenan; Ordered registered.

Deed: James Morriss to Daniel Hicks for 300 acres, proved by Theophilus Williams; Ordered registered.

Deed: Stephen Bearfield to William O'Daniel for 200 acres, proved by Owen O'Daniel; Ordered registered.

Deed: Samuel Ward to William Harris for 200 acres, acknowledged; Ordered registered.

FRIDAY MORNING. Court met at 9 o'clock according to Adjournment.

Present: Worshipfull William Houston,Sr., Thomas Routledge, Joseph Dickson, Esquires.

Ordered Stephen Houseman be recommended to General Assembly for exemption of Taxes & all other Public Duties.

Ordered James McIntire overseer of road from the Cross Roads to Limestone Bridge in room of James Evans & have same hands, also that he work on the River of said district.

Ordered that as the Jury appointed to lay off the road from Outlaws Bridge to Grove Bridge at Thomas Routledges had failed to do so, that the said Jury be again summoned by William McGee, Constable, to meet at the house of Thomas Routledge at such time as William Houston & Thomas Routledge judge expediant for laying off said road.

Ordered Nicholas Hunter & James Middleton (Miller) be added to said Jury & That Samuel Houston attend & qualify said Jury.

Fined William Guy £5 for non attendance this Court as Juryman.

Joseph Dickson returned list of Taxable property for Districts of Capt. Gillispies & Capt. Stallings Companies.

James Lockhart returned list of Taxable property for District of Capt. Wallers Company.

James Kenan returned lists of Taxable property for Districts of Capt. Kenans & Capt. Bowdens Companies.

Samuel Houston returned list of Taxable property for District of Capt. Hubbarts Company.

James Pearsall produced his Commission as Sheriff for the County of Duplin for the present year.

Ordered Joseph Dickson, Samuel Houston, Joseph Grimes & Daniel Glisson be summoned to attend as Jurymen the next Superior Court to be held for the District of Wilmington the 30th of Nov. next.

Joseph Dickson offered as security Thomas Routledge & James McIntire for his guardianship to Mary Williams, orphan of William Williams, dec'd; Approved, bond given of £100.

Allowed James Pearsall, Sheriff, £16 for extra services for 1783.

James Pearsall, being summoned by Jacob Wells as garnishe to render what money or effects he had of property of Samuel Howard, swore that when summoned he had £15 or £20 in notes & accounts as Attorney for Howard which he has since delivered to Howard.

Court Adjourned Till Court in Course.

[signed] William Houston, Sr., Thomas Routledge, Joseph Dickson.

18 January 1785 County Court begun & held for County of Duplin at the Cross Roads, the 3rd Monday.

Present: Worshipfull Thomas Routledge, James Lockhart & Joseph Dickson, Esquires.

Thomas Carleton, William Southerland & William Magee, Constables, summoned to attend this Court.

William Guy, fined for non attendance at last Court, rendered reasons satisfactory to Court; fine remitted.

Joab Blackman who was security for William McClam in three different suits: Jacob Godwin against William McClam, Tho. Thomas against William McClam, Robert Sims against William McClam; delivered William McClam to Court; Ordered Sheriff to take McClam into custody & Blackman discharged.

Ordered James Grimes overseer of road in room of Lavin Watkins.

FRIDAY MORNING, Court met at 9 o'clock according to adjournment.

Present: Worshipfull Thomas Routledge, Joseph Dickson, James Gillispie, James Outlaw, Esquires.

Deed: James Pearsall to Justices of Duplin County for 4 acres for a lot on which to build a Court House, acknowlwdged; Ordered registered.

Ordered County Trustee to pay William Dickson £2-6-0 out of County Tax to reimburse him for two Blank Books, one large bound book for a Minute Docket & one small book for a State Docket.

Allowed William Dickson, Clerk of Court, £15/extra services, for paper, etc. for 1783.

Allowed William Dickson, Clerk of Court, £15 for extra services, paper, etc. for 1784.

William Best, William Kenan & William Southerland, a Committee appointed to settle the estate of William Pearse, dec'd, with Joseph Grimes, Armin'r, reported that Joseph Grimes is indebted to the four orphans of William Pearse £31-6-8 to be equally divided among said orphans to wit:Micajah, Naomi, Ruth, William Alexander Pearse; Ordered report with vouchers filed.

Ordered William Hall finish the bridge he is building over the NorthEast River at Mouth of Limestone by the next Court and shall receive Tolls as follows while he continues to keep the Bridge in good repair:

For every	
Foot Person	£0-0-2
Person & Horse	0-0-4
Cart, Team & Driver	0-1-4
Waggon, Team & Driver	0-2-8
Chair Horse, etc.	0-1-0
4 Wheel Carryette	0-2-0
Led Horse or Work Ox	0-0-2
Head of Neat Cattle	0-0-1
Hog or Sheep	0-0-½

Ordered he keep a copy of these rates set up constantly for Public inspection.

Granted James Pearsall licence to keep a Tavern in his own house, he offered as securities Joseph Dickson & Joseph Grimes.

Court Adjourned till Court in Course, then to meet at James Pearsalls.

[signed] Tho. Routledge, Jo. Dickson, James Gillispie, James Outlaw.

18 April 1785   County Court begun & held for County of Duplin at the house of James Pearsalls, the 3rd Monday.

Present: Worshipfull Thomas Routledge, Joseph Dickson, Joseph Tho. Rhodes, Esquires.

Ordered the following fined for not attending as Jurymen this Court: Thomas James, Aaron Williams, Edward Dickson, William Merrit, Arthur Stokes, John Carr, James Mills, William Rigby, Richard Williams, David Cannon, Jr., William Hooks, Thomas Hill, Richard Meares, William Newton, John Chambers, John Houseman, Jacob Rhodes, William Nethercut, James Bizzel, John Shuffield.

John Murphy granted adm'n of estate of Laughlin Love, dec'd; he offered as securities James Pearsall & William Best & gave bond of £500.

Ordered Tho. Routledge, William Best & Curtis Ivey be a committee to settle estate of Stephen Thomson, dec'd, between James Thomson, Admin'r, & heirs of said dec'd & report end of this Court.

Ordered John Hill have leave to turn the road which leads through his Plantation from Foard of Goshen Swamp to foot of William Kenans path, he making the same as good & convenient for travelers as the road is now.

Ordered Robert Dickson overseer of road from Grove Bridge to the Middle of Run of Maxwell Swamp & have same hands that were under Nicholas Hunter.

Ordered Warrin Blount constable in room of William Moore.

TUESDAY MORNING, Court met at 9 o'clock according to adjournment.

Present: Worshipfull Tho. Routledge, Joseph Dickson, Charles Ward, James Gillispie, Kedar Bryan, Joseph T. Rhodes, Esquires.

Allowed William Moore eight shillings for summoning Inhabitants of his District to give in their Taxables the last year.

Inventory of estate of Ben. Smith, dec'd, exhibited by Joseph T. Rhodes: Ordered filed.

Account of sale of remainder of estate of Thomas Thomson, dec'd, exhibited by James Moore, Admin'r; Ordered filed.

Grand Jury sworn: Thomas James, foreman, Jacob Mathis, Arthur Stokes, John Carr, James Mills, William Rigby, Alexander Dickson, Isaac Thomas, John Farrier, William Wallace, William Hooks, William Newton, John Neale, Joseph Smith, Samuel Rogers.

Ordered Thomas Quin, Constable, attend Grand Jury.

Division of estate of John Moore, dec'd, exhibited by James Kenan, William Dickson & Lavin Watkins; the eleven Negroes were divided equally according to their value amongst the daughters & widow of said dec'd, who, all being of full age, received their legacies & gave receipts; Court concurred & Ordered division filed.

Col. James Moore exhibited an account against the estate of Thomas Thomson, dec'd, amounting to £15 which Court allowed; Ordered filed.

James Thomson, Admin'r of estate of Stephen Thomson, dec'd, exhibited his account against estate; Court approved & Ordered filed.

Ordered Frederick Graddy overseer of road in room of Arthur Herring.

Joab Blackman, security for William McClam in suits of Theophilus Williams vs. William McClam & Stephen King vs. William McClam, surrendered McClam to Court & was discharged.

Joel James, security for William McClam in suits of Jacob Godwin vs. William McClam & Tho's Thomas vs. W. McClam, surrendered McClam & was discharged.

As the Court has received information from members of the last Assembly that sundry Taxes are to be collected & accounted for by the Clerk of the County Courts for which the Clerks are to give bond, etc. & as this Court has never seen the Act for that purpose & Clerk has not given bond as Act has not been published; Ordered that Clerk of this Court receive all Deeds, Conveyances of land, etc. which the Court will order to be recorded & that Clerk will receive on every Deed or Conveyance five shillings Tax & he shall account for five shillings Tax on any Deed or Conveyance of land recorded at last Court, if due by Law at that time; also he shall be liable for every marriage the sum of ten shillings Tax which have been or shall be issued since the last Court till Laws are published & clerk shall have given bond.

Ordered James Maxwell, Charles Ward, William McClam be a Committee to divide the estate of Laughlin Love, dec'd, between heirs of said dec'd & report to next Court.

WEDNESDAY MORNING, Court met at 9 o'clock according to adjournment.

Present: Worshipfull Tho. Routledge, Charles Ward, Kedar Bryan, Joseph T. Rhodes, Dan'l Teachey, James Gillispie, Esquires.

Ordered Thomas Crumpton overseer of road from John Williams to middle of Stewarts Creek Bridge & have same hands belonging to said District & that William Beven, Joseph Beven, Jr., James Knowles, Elias James, Charles James, John Butler, Jeremiah Pearsall, Stephen Williams, John Williams be added to said District & work on said road.

Ordered Frederick Wells overseer of road from John Williams down to middle of Rockfish Bridge & have same hands belonging to said District & all inhabitants of Bull Tail be added to same District.

Read petition of Inhabitants of Rockfish to have navigation of Rockfish opened & cleared from the Bridge up as high as mouth of Fussells Creek.

Ordered Joseph Williams, Sr., Aaron Williams, Joseph Williams, Jr., Peter Newell, Mesheck Stallins, William Duff, Wimbert Boney, Daniel Teachey, Jr., Joseph Beven, John Goff, Sr., Charles James, Jeremiah Pearsall, Thomas Crumpton, Frederick Wells, Edward Dickson, Jacob Wells, Shadrick Stallins, they or a majority be a Committee to view Creek & report to next Court.

Ordered Stephen Rogers be Constable in room of Christopher Martin.

Ordered Thomas Hooks overseer of road in room of Thomas Hill.

Ehibited receipt of Zilpha Pearse to Joseph Grimes, Admin'r of William Pearse, dec'd, for £608-3-3, her distributive share of her said brothers estate; Ordered filed.

Ordered William Hollingsworth overseer of road in room of James Picket.

Ordered William Goff be Constable in room of Thomas Carleton.

Fined William Gully & William Picket twenty shillings for non attendance on Petit Jury; they rendered Court their reason for non attendance; Fine remitted.

THURSDAY MORNING. Court met at 10 o'clock according to adjournment.

Present: Worshipfull Tho. Routledge, Robert Dickson, Joseph Dickson, Charles Ward & James Outlaw, Esquires.

Samuel Albertson, security for defendant in suit of Solomon Goodman vs. Jonathan Taylor, surrendered Taylor to Court & was discharged; Ordered Sheriff to take Taylor into custody.

Allowed Thomas Quin, Constable, 15 shillings for attending Court as constable 3 days.

William Taylor, John Beck, Thomas Gray, Thomas Hooks, George Miller, Joseph Grimes, Daniel Herring, Lewis Thomas & William Dickson, the Committee to report on the practicality of opening the main run of Goshen Swamp for boats, reported that from the abundence of water in the Swamp that it was practical by clearing the main run in dry season; Ordered said Committee to mark & lay off into convenient little Districts from the mouth up as high as the Bridge called Hurst & report the Inhabutants contiguous to said Districts & who they think proper to be overseers in each District.

Ordered Kedar Bryan, Daniel Teachy & David Bunting be a Committee to inspect papers & accounts of Robert Dickson, Esquire relative to the estate of Isom Shuffield, dec'd, & report to this Court.

William Albertson produced deposition of Ann Phillis Bowing & asked to have it recorded; Granted & Order transcribed in minutes, to wit: 9 April 1785. Then An Phillis Bowing came before me, one of the States Justices & made oath on the Holy Evangelist of Almighty God, that her son Elijah Bowen was not 21 years old until the 4th day of June next. Sworn to before me this day, James Outlaw, J.P.

Deed: William Magee to John Magee for 400 acres, proved by John Farrior; Ordered registered.

Deed: James Moore to Thomas Hill for 98 acres, proved by William Dickson; Ordered registered.

Deed: William Graddy to Solomon Carter for 100 acres, proved by Richard Munds; Ordered registered.

Deed: William Allen to Robert Dickson for 300 acres, proved by Cader Harrell; Ordered registered.

Deed: Richard Munds to Edward Carter for 300 acres, acknowledged; Ordered registered.

Deed: Felix Kenan, Sheriff, to Thomas Routledge for 200 acres, acknowledged; Ordered registered.

Deed: Abner Quin to William Nethercut for 100 acres, proved by Caleb Quin; Ordered registered.

Deed: Frederick Glisson to Jesse Brock for 100 acres, proved by John Rogers; Ordered registered.

Deed: Lewis Barnes to Anthony Jones for one piece of land, acknowledged; Ordered registered.

Inventory of estate of Barbara Carr, dec'd, exhibited by William Carr, Admin'r; Ordered filed.

Report of division of estate of Joseph Carr & Barbara Carr, dec'd, rendered by James Maxwell, Robert Dickson & Hugh McCann; Ordered filed.

Thomas Hooks being summoned as garnishee to James McCulloh in suit of Thomas Gray vs. James McCulloh, rendered a bundle of notes, accounts & papers, etc. which he swore was all he then had in his possession of the property of said McCulloh; Ordered they remain in Clerks Office & be subject to judgement on the said attachment when obtained & surplus, if any, be again returned to said James McCulloh or to such persons as may be entitled to receive them.

Ordered that Rich'd Clinton, in Sampson Co., & executors of Edmund Mathis, dec'd, appear at next Court to render account of estate of William Gainey, dec'd; Ordered also that Clerk of this Court bring to Court all papers now in his office relative to said estate.

FRIDAY MORNING, Court met at 9 o'clock according to adjournment.

Present: Worshipfull Tho.Routledge, James Lockhart, James Kenan, James Gillispie, Esquires.

James Kenan last year returned more lands than he was entitled to pay Taxes for; Ordered Collector of Taxes to remit Taxes on 500 acres.

As the Jury to lay off the road from James Outlaws Bridge to Grove Bridge at Col. Routledges & to cross Goshen at the most convenient place, have not convened; Ordered Thomas Routledge, James Gillispie, James Midleton,Sr., Isaac Hunter, William McGowen, James McIntire, John Williams (BC), Edward Pearsall, William Best, William Frederick, James Pearsall, Joseph Dickson, Thomas Hooks, Samuel Ward, William Hall, Robert Southerland, Nicholas Hunter, James Midleton, William Dickson, ~~James Outlaw~~, ~~John Whitehead~~, ~~Daniel Herring~~,~~Stephen Herring~~, they or any 12 of them, be a Jury to lay off said road & report a plan thereof to next Court.

Ordered William Magee, Constable, to convene Jury at house of Joseph Grimes on Goshen & Samuel Houston to qualify Jury.

Kader Bryan, Daniel Teachy, David Bunting, a Committee to settle accounts of Robert Dickson with the estate of Isom Shuffield, dec'd, reported:
His disbursments £128-12-6
Credits 23-17-0
   Balance due Robert Dickson £104-15-6
Ordered report with vouchers filed.

Jacob Padget was charged for Taxes with 530 acres more than he was in possession of; Ordered Collector to remit Taxes for 530 acres for 1784.

Charles Ward was Taxed for 680 acres more than he had in 1784; Ordered Collector to remit.

Jury ordered to lay off a road from James Pearsalls where the Court House now is to the road between Watson Burtons & Limestone did not agree; Ordered Ephram Garrison, James Dickson, James McIntire, John Mallard, Joseph Smith, Benja. Dulaney, Nath'l McCann, Robert Williams, James Mills, Stephen Rogers, James Maxwell, John Best,Sr., Phill Southerland, Richard Chasen, they or any 12, be a Committee to lay off said road & report to next Court.

Deed: Theophilus Swinson to John Matchet for 250 acres, proved by Charles Ward; Ordered registered.

Ordered Samuel Houston be overseer of NorthEast River from William Kernegays Bridge down to James Rogers landing & have the following hands: Peter Hall, Thomas Welch, John Southerland, Anth'y Millers Will, Frederick Smith, Charles Miller, Edward Houston, Doctor Houstons Ned, John Neale,Jr., Jacob Williams, Stephen Miller, John New, Clement Godfrey, David Greear, John Houseman, William Kernegay, Lewis Barns Boson, Sam'l Jones,Jr., John Williams Negro, Thomas Shelton, James Williams,Jr. , John Brock, Stephen Gufford, Arthur Herrings Will.

Account of additional sale of estate of Herald Blackmore, dec'd, exhibited by Felix Kenan; Ordered registered.

Ordered Robert Twilley be overseer of the River from James Rogers landing down to the Indian Graves with the following hands: Nathan Fountain, Henry Fountain, Benja. Lanier, John Lanier, William Southerland, William New, Jeremiah Williams, Nicho's Fennel, Nicholas Sandlin, John Magee & his Negro Cogdell, Henry Newkirk, Thomas Canaday, Ebenezar Garrison, Leonard Mills, Cato Mills, Mingo Mills, James Cox, Phil Southerland, March'l Burdoo, James Midleton, Deny McIntire, Gillispie Lam, Dickson & McGowens Negroes Sip & Potter.

Appointed Nathaniel McCann overseer of the River from the Indian Graves down to the Mouth of Rockfish & have the following hands: Martin Hanchy, Moses Hanchy, John Whitman, Jesse Norris, William McCann, William Picket, James Murray & his Negro Sam, Abel Rogers, Solomon Cox, Wm. Sholder, Charles Goff, Jacob Hollingsworth, James Hollingsworth, James Lanier.

Appointed James Gillispie, Robert Dickson & Joseph Thomas Rhodes a Committee to inspect the NorthEast River from the Mouth of Rockfish up to William Kernegays Bridge above Mouth of Goshen Swamp & to direct & superintend the Overseer of River & report from time to time the order the River is in & whether Overseer does his duty.

James Gray recordrd his mark: 2 swallow forks.

Thomas Gray recorded his mark: 1 swallow fork in left ear & an uper slope in right ear.

Petition of sundry Inhabitants of NE Swamp to have cleared the run of NE as high as James Outlaws; Ordered James Outlaw, William Graddy, Michael Glisson, Frederick Bearfield, Arthur Herring, Daniel Herring, Lutson Stroud, James Mathews, Richard Munds be a Committee to view said run & report to next Court.

Ordered John Molten, James Midleton, Sr., James Dickson, William Frederick, James Heath, Geo. Mallard, William Stokes, Ephram Garrison, Thomas Carleton, Elias James, Joseph Bevan,Sr., Joseph Williams (RF), John Avers, John Cook (IC), Jeremiah Williams, Abraham Newkirk, John Magee, Nathan Waller, John Lanier, Benja. Lanier, Daniel Hicks, Benja. Johnston, Samuel Guy, Hancock Hatcher, Anthony Miller, William Hubbard, Absalom Mercer, William Thomson, Wm. Kernegay, Stephen Herring, Mich'l Glisson, Samuel Bowden, John Rogers, John Hill, Samuel Boyd, Richard Cooper, George Miller be Jurymen for next Court.

Ordered Joseph Dickson, James Gillispie, Joseph T.Rhodes, Theophilus Williams be Jurors to next Superior Court to be held at Wilmington June 6th next.

Account of sales of estate of Stephen Cade, dec'd, exhibited by Sheriff; Ordered filed.

Allowed Thomas Carleton, Constable, twenty shillings for serving as constable 4 days at last October Court, also twenty shillings for 4 days at January Court.

Allowed William Magee, Constable, fifteen shillings for 3 days at last July Court, also twenty shillings for 4 days this Court.

Ordered Benjamin Johnston be overseer of road from where the County line crosses the road between the Old Court House & Turkey to where said line crosses the road below Daniel Hicks & also from the Old Court House to Stewarts Creek near John Moltens & have the hands in said District.

Ordered James Midleton, Sr., be overseer in room of John Armstrong.

Ordered Lewis Hines be overseer of road in room of Michael Glisson.

Nicholas Routledge, one of the Collectors of Taxes for 1784, rendered a list of Insolvents amounting to £8-9-10 in money & £5-6-0 in Tickets; Ordered list filed & said sums allowed him in his settlement with the Sheriff.

Account of sales of estate of Thankful Hicks, dec'd, exhibited; Ordered filed.

Ordered the Clerk made deductions of several allowances for Insolvents & errors which were allowed & same be deducted before amount of Taxes be returned to Treasurer or Sheriff.

Inventory of estate of Virginia Coppersmith, dec'd, exhibited by James Gillespie, Admin'r; Ordered filed.

Court Adjourned Till Court in Course.

[signed] Tho. Routledge, James Gillespie, Kedar Bryan, Robert Dickson, Joseph Dickson, Sam'l Houston.

18 July 1785 County Court begun & held for County of Duplin, the 3rd Monday.

Present: Worshipfull Thomas Routledge, James Kenan, Joseph Dickson, Charles Ward, Kedar Bryan, Joseph T. Rhodes, Esquires.

Joseph Godwin, Special Bail & Security for William Laiton in suit of William McClam vs. William Laiton, surrendered Laiton to Court & was discharged.

John Bryan, Special Bail & Security for William Laiton in suit of William McClam vs. William Laiton, surrendered Laiton to Court & was discharged.

Inventory of estate of Peter Barbree, dec'd, exhibited by Peggy Barbree, Exe'rx; Ordered filed.

Ordered John Parker be constable in room of Charles Goff.

Read petition that Joseph William, an aged & infirm man, be recommended to General Assembly as an object to be exempted from payment of Taxes infuture as a Poll Taxable person; Granted.

Grand Jury sworn: John Molten, foreman, James Dickson, Ephram Garrison, William Hubbard, William Stokes, Absalom Marcus, James Midleton, Sr., William Kornegay, John Rogers, Ben Johnston, John Lanier, George Mallard, Joseph Beven, Rich'd Cooper, Anthony Miller.

Ordered Stephen Rogers, Constable, attend Grand Jury.

Daniel Glisson, one of the Collectors of Taxes for 1784, rendered a list of Insolvents which Court allowed, to wit:

	Gen. Tax	County	Parish	Ct.House	Goal
Rawley Mills	£0-16-0	1/4	1/4	1/4	/10d
Patrick Norris				1/	/ 4d
William Hurst				2/2	1/ 1d
Isaac Hurst	0-12-0	1/	1/	1/	1/ 4d
John V. Taylor	0-16-0	1/4	1/4	1/4	/ 8d
Ward Ward	0-16-0	1/4	1/4	1/4	/ 8d
Elijah Wiggins	0-12-0	1/	1/	1/	/ 4d
John Carroll	?-16-0	3/	3/	3/	1/ 6d
	£5- 8-0	9	9	12/2	5/11

Sheriff having settled Taxes with Treasurer for 1784 & paid same; Ordered said Daniel Glisson be allowed above sum at time of settling & paying of his Taxes for 1785, also Daniel Glisson allowed remitance of Taxes on 400 acres which was allowed in favor of Col. Kenan

		1/8	1/8	1/8	/10
	£5- 8-0	10/8	10/8	10/8	6/9

William Kenan granted admin'n on estate of Felix Kenan, dec'd, offered as securities John Molten, John Hill, Thomas Hill & Charles Ward; gave bond of £3,000.

TUESDAY MORNING, Court met at 8 o'clock according to adjournment.

Present: Worshipfull Thomas Routledge, James Lockhart, Joseph Dickson, John Beck, Kedar Bryan, Esquires.

Will of David Sloan, dec'd, exhibited & proved by Robert Sloan & Jacob Beverit; Margaret Sloan, Lewis Brock & David Sloan qualified as executors.

James Holland granted admin'n on estate of William Dobson, dec'd, offered as securities William Hubbard & Sam'l Jones, gave bond of £150.

Ordered Solomon Whitehead, Orphan age 12 on 16 April last, son of Elizabeth Whitehead, bound apprentice to Stephen Rogers till age 21, to learn the trade of Sadler & to read & write & cypher as far as the rule of three.

Noncupative Will of William Thomson, dec'd, Exhibited, proved & attested by James Outlaw; Ordered filed.

Ordered Elizabeth Thomson, widow of said dec'd, have admin'n on unwilled part of estate; she offered as securities William Hubbard & Samuel Houston; gave bond of £200.

The election of Sheriff came on; present were William Houston, Tho. Routledge, Robert Dickson, James Lockhart, Joseph Dickson, John Wright, Charles Ward, Sam'l Houston, John Beck, James Gillespie, Kedar Bryan, Joseph T. Rhodes, James Outlaw who elected the Hon. James Kenan Sheriff for ensuing year.

Ordered Samuel Houston, William Hubbard & James Outlaw be a Committee to divide the estate of William Thomson, dec'd, the undivided part, between the Widow & Orphans & report to next Court.

Nicholas Hunter recorded his mark: a smooth crop in left ear & an under slope in right ear.

William Ball & William Best, Special Bail & Security for William McClam in suit of Theoph's Williams vs. William McClam, surrendered McClam to Court; Thomas Gray acknowledged himself Special Bail for McClam in said suit.

Ordered Rich'd Matthews constable in room of William Goff.

Ordered Lewis Hines overseer of road in room of Michael Glisson.

James Kenan produced Commission signed by Gov. Caswell appointing him Sheriff of the County; gave bond.

William Dickson, Clerk of Court, gave bond of £1,000 with appropriate security for the performance of the several duties of his office; bond in hands of Wm. Houston.

WEDNESDAY MORNING, Court met at 9 o'clock according to adjournment.

Present: Worshipfull William Houston, Thomas Routledge, Joseph Dickson, John Beck, Kedar Bryan, Esquires.

Inventory of estate of Thankfull Hicks exhibited, proved by James Mills; Ordered filed.

Ordered Joseph Wetts discharged from payment of Taxes on Negro Jim until Court adjudge Negro restored to health.

Ordered Thomas Jernigan, an aged,blind man, be recommended to General Assembly as an object to be exempted from paying Poll Tax.

Ordered Frederick Graddy overseer of road in room of Arthur Herring.

Ordered Jonathan Parker, Daniel Parker, Peter Parker, Solomon Dobson & Demsey Taylor added to District & work on road where Frederick Bearfield is Overseer.

Granted Isaac Hunter licence to keep an Ordinary or Tavern at his own house; offered as securities Thomas Gray & James Pearsall & gave bond of £100.

Thomas Routledge granted licence to keep an Ordinary or Tavern at his own house; offered Edward Pearsall & James Murrow as securities & gave bond of £100.

Thos. Atkinson, ward of Henry Hollingsworth, alledged that he was 21 years of age; Ordered Hollingsworth to answer at next Court for his guardianship of said ward & also for guardianship of Mary Atkinson.

Ordered Clerk bring to Court all papers relative to estate of John Atkinson, dec'd.

William Kenan as garnishee in suit now pending of Alexander Laine vs. Henry Eustace McCulloh, said all property of McCulloh which was in his custody was filed in Clerks office.

Grand Jury returned list of Orphans; Ordered persons who had custody of said Orphans render account at next Court.

Ordered late Sheriff, James Pearsall, be allowed £20 for extra services last year.

THURSDAY MORNING, Court met at 9 o'clock according to adjournment.

Present: Worshipfull William Houston, Robert Dickson, James Lockhart, Samuel Houston, John Beck, Esquires.

Ordered Fred'k Smith exempted from Tax for his Negro Abraham who is aged & unable to labor.

Ordered Samuel Houston overseer of River from William Kernegays Bridge down to James Rogers landing and have the following hands: Peter Hall, Thomas Welch, John Southerland,

Anthony Millers Will, Frederick Smith, Charles Miller, Edward
Houston, Doctor Houstons Ned, John Neale, Jr., John Houseman,
William Kernegay, Arthur Herrings Will, Lewis Bames Boson &
Peter, Samuel Jones, Jr., John Williams Negro, Tho. Shelton,
James Williams, Jr., Mills Mumford, Charles Sewell, William
Pennington, Moses Conner, Anthony Jones & George Williams
Negro Will.

Ordered William McCann, Jr. & his Negro Harry, Hugh McCann,
Jr., Aaron Hodgeson, Joseph Hodgeson & Widow Murrows Negro
added to lower District of River & work under Nathaniel McCann.

Ordered Tax of 1/ levied on every Poll Taxable Person & on
every 300 acres to discharge the Contingencies of this County.

Ordered Rockfish Creek cleared from Mouth up to Mouth of
Fussells Creek, that Joseph Williams be overseer & have the
following hands: Charles James, James Knowles, Elias James,
Stephen Williams, Joseph Williams, Jr., Britton Powell, James
Bland, Edw'd Dicksons 2 Negroes, Timothy Murphys 2 Negroes,
John Goff, Jr., William Bryan, David Williams, Joseph Williams
Negroes, William Goff, Simon Rivenbark, David Davis & George
Willis.

The Committee appointed last Court to view the run of the
NE River from Wm. Kernegays Bridge as high as James Outlaws,
reported that said River is navigatable for boats to pass &
repass; Ordered said run cleared from William Kernegays
Bridge up to James Outlaws Bridge.

Ordered Samuel Sowell overseer of NE River from William
Kernegays Bridge up to Solomon Carters footway & have hands
that worked under him on the road & to proceed immediately
to clear said run & report to next Court.

Ordered Lewis Hines overseer of the NE River from Solomon
Carters footway up to Outlaws Bridge & have the hands belong-
ing to his own & Jas. Mathews companies, except John Mainer
& Besent Brock.

The Committee appointed last Court to lay off run of Goshen
Swamp into convenient small Districts, have laid off said run
from Mouth to Mouth of Panther Swamp; Court approved Overseers
& hands as follows:
1st District, from Mouth up to a marked tree with one notch
including Millers foard: Stephen Miller, overseer, George
Millers 2 Negroes, Richard Roberts, Henry Shehon, Joseph
Wetts Negro Jim, John Chambers Negro Captain, James Chambers
Negroes June & Dick, Flud Foley, Elizabeth Foleys son Jeremiah
& all others belonging to said families;
2nd District, from marked tree up run to a gum tree marked
with two notches, including Chambers foard: John Matchet,
overseer, John New, Clement Godfrey, Joseph Bray, John Johnston
& his Negro Boson, David Greear, Rich'd Swinson, Absalom
Swinson & Negro Jo, Theophilus Swinson, Auston Swinson, [blank]

Mizel, Jacob Williams, Samuel Williams, John Best,Jr. & John Platt & all others in their families;

3rd District, from tree marked with 2 notches up the run to lower end of Matchets Slew: Stephen Herring, overseer, Benja. Herring, William Kenans 2 Negroes at his Quarter, Jacob Glisson, John Glisson, Andrew Guffords 2 sons Stephen & James, Arthur Herring, Jr., Whitfield Herring, Alexander Herring, Daniel Herrings Negro Tom, Benjamin Snipes, John Brock, Demsey Goff, William Mainer, John Mainer & all hands in their families;

4th District, from lower end of Matchets Slew up to Gavins old foard & including Gavins Slew: Joseph Grimes, overseer, Joseph Grimes 2 sons & their Negroes, Edw'd Sloan, Charles Wards 4 Negroes, Charles Brown, Robert Williams,Jr., Charles George Tilman, Lemon Dunn, Uriah Gurganus, David Quin, James Quin, George Quin, Robert Williams,Sr. & his son & Negroes & all others belonging to their families;

5th District, from Gavins old foard up the main run to lower end of Herrings Slew or with the main run to a new marked path between Dan'l Herrings & Joseph Grimes: Sampson Grimes, overseer, Rubin Weston, Jr., John Sulliven, Nathan Bullard, Caleb Sulliven, Michael Sulliven, Jethro Mainer, Alexander Sanders, Widow Sullivens Negro, John Whitehead, James Grimes, William Sulliven, Besent Brock & all other hands in their families;

6th District, from lower end of Herrings Slew or from the new path between Daniel Herrings & Joseph Grimes up to lower end of Ward Great Slew: David Cannon, overseer, John Aaron, John Best, Sr. & his 2 sons Howell & Benjamin, Matthew Gainey, George Cooper, Jr. & his Negro, Richard Cooper, William Kenans Negroes supposed to be 10, James Fleming, T.Jernigans Negro & all others belonging to their families;

7th District, from lower end of Wards Great Slew up to the uper end of Sampson Grimes Slew: William Sulliven, overseer, John Hills 3 Negroes, Edward Harris, Lewis Thomas 2 Negroes, Jonathan Thomas, William Sullivens Negro, James Ward, Noell Pennington, Christopher Martin, John Fleming, George Cooper,Sr. & his Negro & his son, James Winders & all others belonging to their families;

8th District, from uper end of Sampson Grimes Slew to head of Outlaws Slew: John Sulliven, overseer, Owen Sulliven, John Winders,Jr., Edward Winders, John Winders 3 Negroes, John Swinsons Negro Bristo, John Rogers, Jr., William Rogers, Solomon Rogers, Micajah Rogers, Jesse Brock, William Taylors 2 Negroes, Joshua Chambles, Samuel Bowden, James Stone, Jesse Swinson & all others belonging to their families;

9th District, from head of Outlaws Slew up to John Hills foard: William Hooks, overseer, William Hooks Negro, Thomas Phipps, William Phipps, Thomas Phipps, Jr., Thomas Hooks, Jr., John Cha. Slocumb, Tho. Hooks, Sr. & his 2 Negroes, Charles Hooks, Richard Singleton, Richard Meares, Thomas Hill his 6 Negroes, Owen Tyler & all others belonging to their families;

10th District, from Hills foard up to Winders foot path including Sullivens Slew: James Wright, overseer, Thomas Wright, Patrick Newton & his 2 Negroes, James Guy, Robert Wilkinson his

Negro & William Wilkinson, James Moore, Jacob Monk, William Newton, John Newton, Rubin Cook, Felix Frederick & all others belonging to their families;

11th District, from Winders foot path up to lower end of Rogers Slew: Lavin Watkins, overseer, Lavin Watkins Negro, Isaac Spence, John Gibbs, Jr., Elisha Gibbs, Mark Rogers, Geo. Outlaw, Solomon Singar, Richard Bradley, John Shuffield, Ephram Shuffield, Hardy Reeves, Francis Olliver & his Negro, Elisha Jernigan, Nicholas Bowden, Samuel Bowden,Jr., Baker Bowden & all others belonging to their families;

12th District, from lower end of Rogers Slew to lower end of Foleys Slew: Theophilus Williams, overseer, Ben Ezel, Theo Williams 2 Negroes, Wm. Guy, Fred'k Homes, Luke Ward, Jr., James White, John Ward, Jr., [blank] Timmons, Cullen Connerly, William Ward, Philip Ward, Warrin Blount, John McCallop, Ben Blount, John Stuckeys 2 Negroes, Lewis Stuckey & all others belonging to their families;

13th District, from lower end of Foleys Slew to uper end of Cannons Slew: Daniel Glisson, overseer, Daniel Glissons Negro Toney, John Hart, John Wright,Jr.s Negroes Durham & Kitt, Stephen Herring,Jr. & Negro Cesar, William Ward, William Pollock, Sam'l Ward, Jesse Grants Negroes Philip & Cesar, David Cannon, George Gaylor & a Negro, William Dickson his 4 Negroes & all others belonging to their families;

14th District, from head of Cannons Slew to opposite Mouth of White Oak & Wards Branch: Willis Cherry, overseer, James Bizzel, William Stone, Arthur Bizzel, Hardy Bizzel & a Negro, Thomas Bennet, William Bennet, Samuel Bennet, Jacob Millard, Isaac Millard, Hezekiah Millard, Moses Branch, Dred Branch, William Taylor, John Wade, William Underhill, Hardy Daniel, Aaron Daniel & all others belonging to their families;

15th District, from Mouth of White Oak up to the Bridge: John Bradley, overseer, Jephtha Daniel, James Bradley, Shadrick Daniel, John Daniel,Jr., William Gully & his son, Thomas Wiggins & his Negro, William Burnham, William Hurst & his 2 Negroes, James Harrell, James Oates & his Negro, Thomas Flowers, Simon Flowers, Starling Powell & all others belonging to their families;

16th District, from the Bridge up to Mouth of Reedy Branch: Hillary Hooks, overseer, Henry Faison & his 6 Negroes, John Griffin, Micajah Byrd, Daniel Byrd, Robert Byrd,Jr. & Negro Toney, Shadrick Byrd, John Clark, Daniel Clark, James Clark, Patrick McCanne, Doctor Frazars 2 Negroes, Micajah Frazar, James Frazar & all others belonging to their families;

17th District, from Mouth of Reedy Branch up to the Bluff above Mouth of Panther: William Beck, overseer, John Beck, Jr.s Negroes, Stephen Beck, Stephen Snell & his Negro, William Stephens 2 sons & 3 Negroes, Nathaniel Kinnard, John Haines, William Simpler, Amos Walker, Thomas Gray & his 4 Negroes & all others belonging to their families.

Ordered Swamp of Goshen be divided into 3 Divisions, each Superintended by three Commissioners authorized & impowered by the Court to direct & instruct the several overseers in each of their respective Districts,to shew them their several places & to report to Court from time to time as to how work is carried on & what further necessary for Court to direct, said Commissioners, or any two, may appoint another overseer in case an overseer shall remove or refuse to act, & said overseer shall have same power & authority until next Court as though he were appointed by the Court.

Ordered George Miller, Daniel Herring & Joseph Grimes superintendants of lower division, from Mouth of Goshen up to lower end of Wards Slew, including six Districts.

Ordered William Taylor, Thomas Hooks & Lewis Thomas superintendants of middle District, from lower end of Wards Slew up to lower end of Foleys Slew, including six Companies.

Ordered John Beck, Thomas Gray & William Dickson superintendants of uper division, from lower end of Foleys Slew up to Bluff above Mouth of Panther, including five companies.

Ordered all hands compelled to work on Goshen Swamp by order of this Court exempted from working on roads this year, except repairing of Bridges, such as Soracta Bridge, Goshen Bridge & the Bridges & Causeways crossing the principal branches running into Goshen Swamp on either side.

As the Jury appointed to lay off the road from Outlaws Bridge on the NorthEast to Grove Bridge at Col. Routledges & to cross Goshen at the best & Most convenient place has not been convened, Ordered that Thomas Routledge, James Gillispie, James Midleton, Sr., Isaac Hunter, William McGowen, James McIntire, John Williams (B.C.), Edward Pearsall, William Best, William Frederick, James Pearsall, Joseph Dickson, Thomas Hooks, Samuel Ward, William Hall, Robert Southerland, Nicho's Hunter, James Midleton, Jr., Wm. Dickson, James Dickson, James Jackson [?], James Evens, they or any twelve be a Jury to lay off said road & report to next Court.

Ordered William Magee, Constable, convene said Jury at house of Thomas Routledge on Monday, August 1, next & William Houston qualify said Jury.

Ordered John Wright take list of Taxables in room of James Kenan & return same to next Court.

James Kenan, Sheriff, protests against Goal as insufficient to hold any prisoner; Ordered recorded.

Ordered road leading from Kinnards Bridge on Goshen to Aaron Martins on Thunder Swamp be continued where it was first laid off & opened & that John Beck be Overseer & also old road leading from Kinnards Bridge to Old School House at County line towards Buck Swamp be under him & he have same hands on same roads as formerly.

Appointed James Kenan & Charles Ward guardians to William Matchet, minor Orphan of John Matchet, dec'd; Ordered they give Bond of £1,000.

Daniel Hicks & James Dickson appoined Inspectors & Assistants in taking votes of Electers at next ensueing election on 3rd Friday & Saturday in August next.

Inventory & Account of Sales of Estate of Laughlin Love, dec'd, exhibited by Sheriff; Ordered filed.

Granted William Houston licence to keep an Ordinary or Tavern at his Plantation at Soracta, he offered as securities William Hall & Edward Pearsall & gave Bond.

Ordered Thomas James, Wimbert Boney, Nathaniel Edwards, Shadrick Stallins, Auston Beesley, Robert Southerland, Nathan Fountain, Henry Newkirk, Joab Fountain, Lott Gregory, George Smith, Sr., John Williams (B.C.), John Sulliven, Stephen Gufford, Stephen Herring, Lewis Hines, James McIntire, James Evens, James Midleton, Jr., John Cox, James Carr, Stephen Miller, John Johnston, Jr., Ivey Smith, John Gow, David Cannon, Jr., Samuel Ward, Dan'l Glisson, Stephen Snell, Thomas Flowers, William Duncan, Rubin Johnston, William Harris serve as Jurors at next Court.

Deed: Andrew Wallace to Timothy Murphy for 58 acres, acknowledged; Ordered registered.

Deed: James Pearsall & wife to James James for 2 pieces of land, 45 acres, acknowledged; Ordered registered.

Deed: Adam Platt to Moses Hanchy for 100 acres, acknowledged; Ordered registered.

Deed: James Williams to Austin Beesley for 50 acres, proved by Solomon Beesley; Ordered registered.

Deed: Jonathan Davis to David Davis for 50 acres, proved by Joseph Dickson; Ordered registered.

Deed: William Routledge & Easter Routledge to Edward Pearsall for 251 acres, proved by James Pearsall; Ordered registered.

Deed: John Cook to Emanuel Bowzer for 250 acres, proved by Joseph Dickson; Ordered registered.

Deed: James Evens to George Mallard for 50 acres, proved by James Dickson; Ordered registered.

Deed: Abraham Beesley to Thomas Heath for 83 acres, proved by James Heath; Ordered registered.

Deed: Richard Williams to Abraham Andrews for 100 acres, proved by Nicholas Fennell; Ordered registered.

Deed: William Stokes to Major Croom for 72 acres, acknowledged; Ordered registered.

Deed: Stephen Williams to Abraham Andrews for 50 acres, proved by Nicholas Fennell; Ordered registered.

Deed: Frederick Bearfield to Andrew Gufford for 100 acres, acknowledged; Ordered registered.

Deed: John Parker to Joseph Beven for 100 acres, proved by Joseph Beven; Ordered registered.

Deed: Richard Williams to Jeremiah Williams for 75 acres, proved by Joseph Willson; Ordered registered.

Deed: Abraham Beesley to Joseph Willson for 100 acres, proved by James Wallace; Ordered registered.

Deed: James Wallace to Joseph Wilson for 180 acres, acknowledged; Ordered registered.

Deed: Joseph Willson to James Wallace for 250 acres, acknowledged; Ordered registered.

Deed: Henry Hollingsworth to Hardy Carrol for 196 acres, proved by Arthur Mathews; Ordered registered.

Deed: From Jacob Fussell by Timothy Bloodworth, his Attorney, for 360 acres, proved by John Duff; Ordered registered. [no Grantee named]

Deed: Lewis Graddy to William Whitfield for 148 acres, acknowledged; Ordered registered.

Deed: Abraham Kornegay to William Whitfield for 200 acres, proved by Bryan Whitfield; Ordered registered.

Deed: Robert Merrit to Andrew Neeley for lands, acknowledged; Ordered registered.

Deed: William Southerland to Henry Newkirk for 75 acres, proved by Daniel Southerland; Ordered registered.

Deed: James Maxwell to James McIntire for 300 acres, acknowledged; Ordered registered.

FRIDAY MORNING, Court met at 9 o'clock according to adjournment.

Present: Worshipfull William Houston, Thomas Routledge, Robert Dickson, Joseph Dickson, James Gillespie, Joseph T. Rhodes, Esquires.

Power of Attorney from Michael Dickson to Robert Dickson proved by William Dickson; Ordered registered.

Ordered that John Smith, aged & poor man, unable to get his living by his labor, be recommended to General Assembly as an object to be exempted from Taxes for himself as a Poll.

Ordered that as lists of Taxables have not been returned agreeable to Order of last Court, that said Justices proceed to take lists of Taxables in their Districts & return same to next Court.

Ordered James Pearsall, James Dickson & James McIntire be Searchers for District of Capt. Gillespies Company the ensueing year.

Court Adjourned Till Court in Course.

[signed] William Houston, Sr., Tho. Routledge, Joseph Dickson, Robert Dickson, J.T. Rhodes, James Gillespie.

17 October 1785 County Court Begun & Held for County of Duplin at the Court House, the 3rd Monday.

Present: Worshipfull Thomas Routledge, Joseph Dickson, Samuel Houston, James Gillespie, Esquires.

Ordered that as Thomas Carrol, Orphan & son of Thomas Carrol, dec'd, proved himself to be 21 years of age & prayed for recovery of his part of his fathers estate, that Clerk furnish him with transcript of all records, papers, inventories, sales, etc. of said estate which may be found in Clerks office.

Willis Bass & Joel Williams, Securities & Special Bail for William Laiton in suit of William McClam vs. Wm Laiton, surrendered Laiton to Court; Ordered Sheriff to take him into custody & he is in Sheriffs custody; released by Plaintiffs Attorney.

Ordered Jasper Cox, Orphan 12 years old the 15th of last June, bound apprentice to Nicholas Sandlin till age 21, to learn trade of Shoemaker & to read & write & cypher as far as the Rule of three.

TUESDAY MORNING, Court met at 9 o'clock according to adjournment.

Present: Worshipfull William Houston, Thomas Routledge, Joseph Dickson, Charles Ward, James Gillespie, Kedar Bryan, Daniel Teache[y], Esquires.

Will of Daniel Alderman proved by Robert Rollins & Joshua Lee; David Alderman & Daniel Alderman, Executors named in said Will, qualified.

John Cook, one of executors of John Cook, dec'd, Qualified as Executor.

Ordered Daniel McCallop, Orphan, bound apprentice to David Murdock until age 21, to learn trade of Taylor & to read & write.

Exhibited deposition of Jonathan Taylor taken before Thomas Routledge & James Gillespie proving his insolvency; Ordered filed.

Inventory of estate of James Green, dec'd, exhibited & proved by Rachel Hogans, Admin'x; Ordered filed.

Inventory of estate of Daniel Alderman, dec'd, exhibited; Ordered filed.

Grand Jury sworn: Thomas James, foreman, James Carr, Stephen Gufford, James Midleton, Rubin Johnston, James Evens, John Cox, Henry Newkirk, William Dunkin, Nathan Fountain, Shadrick Stallins, Robert Southerland, Stephen Miller, John Johnston, Jr., Lewis Hines, David Cannon.

Ordered Warrin Blount, Constable, attend Grand Jury.

Ordered Mrs. Elizabeth Gray, executor of John Gray, dec'd, sell some horses & make return to next Court.

Ordered Mary Spears, a widow woman, seited to attend next Court & produce her orphan children, as it is suggested to this Court that they are in a suffering condition.

John Matchet, Security & Special Bail for defendant in suit of William O'Daniel vs. John Smith, surrendered the principal to Court; Ordered Sheriff to take him into custody.

Ordered Bird Lanier, a poor & cripple man, having no property & unable to get his living by labour, be recommended to General Assembly as an object to be exempted from payment of Taxes.

Inventory of estate of David Sloan, dec'd, exhibited & proved by David Sloan, Admin'r; Ordered filed.

Inventory of estate of Wm. Thomson, dec'd, exhibited: Ordered filed.

Account of sales of estate of William Thomson, dec'd, exhibited; Ordered filed.

Inventory of estate of William Dobson, dec'd, exhibited; Ordered filed.

Account of sale of estate of William Dobson, dec'd, exhibited; Ordered filed.

Roger Snell exhibited account against estate of Stephen Thomson, dec'd, amounting to £12-0-0; Ordered he be allowed $19 & no more & that Admin'r pay same; Ordered said account filed.

Inventory of estate of William Jones, dec'd, exhibited; Ordered filed.

Allowed Warrin Blount 16 shillings for attending Court two days as Constable.

Solomon Mainer, Orphan, at last Court was bound apprentice to Stephen Rogers by the name of Solomon Whitehead & it appearing that the Court was induced thereto by false suggestions of said Stephen Rogers, Ordered said Solomon Mainer released from his indentures & discharged from his apprenticeship with Stephen Rogers & that Rogers surrender him to John Whitehead who is required to receive him.

Ordered Elisha Jernigan be Constable in room of Arthur Bizell.

William Laiton, being in custody of the Sheriff at the suit of William McClam, is released by order of Plaintiffs Attorney.

WEDNESDAY MORNING. Court met at 9 o'clock according to adjournment.

Present: Worshipfull William Houston, Tho. Routledge, Robert Dickson, Joseph Dickson, Kedar Bryan, Esquires.

John Wright returned his list of Taxables; Ordered filed.

Joseph Dickson returned his list of Taxables; Ordered filed.

Inventory of estate of Felix Kenan, dec'd, exhibited; Ordered filed.

Allowed Stephen Rogers 32 shillings for attending Court four days as Constable.

Read petition of sundry inhabitants of Rockfish praying to have a road laid off from junction of Duplin & Sampson Counties with New Hanover County at Bulltail Branch to the Court House, to cross Rockfish Creek first at old foard below John Goff,Jr. & next at Bowens old foard below Tim. Murphys & join the road at or near Edward Dicksons or at most convenient or usefull place; Granted & Ordered Shadrick Stallins, Edward Dickson, John Goff,Sr., John Goff, Jr., Abraham Newton, Hardy Powell, Joseph Beven, Sr., Frederick Williams, William Beven, Elijah Bowen, Thomas Crumpton, Nathaniel Edwards, Joshua Edwards, William Goff, William Murphy, or any 12, be a jury to lay off said road & report a plan to next Court.

Ordered Rice Matthis, Constable, to convene said jury at Edward Dicksons & notify Kedar Bryan to attend & qualify said jury.

Appointed Frederick Bearfield collector of all Taxes in Districts of Capt. Whiteheads, Capt. Millers & Capt. Hubbards Companies, he gave bond with approved security of £2,000.

Ordered Joab Padget be overseer of road in room of George Cooper & have his hands that were left off the Swamp.

Ordered William Kenan, garnishee in suit of Alexander Laine against Henry Eustace McCulloh, retain a sum of property of said McCulloh sufficient to indemnify him against Bond entered into by Felix Kenan to Joseph Herring for £50 with interest thereon.

Appointed Thomas Wright collector of all Taxes in whole District of Capt. Kenans & Capt. Bowdens Companies, he gave bond with approved security of £1,000.

Appointed William Wells collector of all Taxes in whole District of Capt. Gillespies, Capt. Stallins & Capt. Southerlands Companies, he gave bond with security of £1,000.

Ordered Joseph Dickson, Samuel Houston, James Lockhart & Isaac Hunter be jurymen to next Superior Court at Wilmington, December 6th next.

James Lockhart returned his list of Taxables.

Ordered following to next Court to render accounts of Orphans in their possession: Ann Henderson, 3; Mary Shears, 3; Priscilla Burris, 6; Hannah Batts, 3; Sarah Batts, 4; William Allen or his wife, 9; Ruth Coggin, 1; John Tucker, 1; Sarah Allen, 2.

THURSDAY MORNING, Court met at 9 o'clock according to adjournment.

Present: Worshipfull Thomas Routledge, Robert Dickson, Joseph Dickson, Charles Ward, James Gillespie, Kedar Bryan, Esquires.

Charles Ward returned his list of Taxables, Ordered filed.

Samuel Houston returned his list of Taxables, Ordered filed.

Ordered William Moore, wounded soldier who served as Sargeant in the Continental Army, be recommended to General Assembly for an allowance of £8 for 1785.

Ordered James Roberts have admin'n on estate of Jesse Roberts, dec'd; he gave bond of £200 & took oath of Administration.

Ordered Charles James be overseer of Rockfish Creek from Mouth up to Bridge & have following hands: James Knowles, John Wilson, Simon Wood, Simon Rivenbark, Lott Green, William Knowles & one hand from Edward Dickson & one hand from Tim Murphy.

Ordered remainder of hands appointed last Court to work on Rockfish Creek under Joseph Williams to return to Districts under Overseers where they formerly belonged.

Exhibited account current with James Gillespie against estate of Edward John James Augustus Carter, dec'd, attested to; Ordered filed.

Ordered Loftis Worley constable in room of Joseph Bray.

FRIDAY MORNING. Court met at 9 o'clock according to adjournment.

Present: Worshipfull William Houston, Thomas Routledge, Robert Dickson, Joseph Dickson, Charles Ward, James Gillespie, Esquires.

Deed: Robert Dickson to Martin Rouse for 100 acres, acknowledged; Ordered registered.

Deed: Ruban Green to Frederick Williams for 90 acres, proved by James Ryan; Ordered registered.

Deed: Thomas Crumpton to David Hall for 150 acres, proved by Joseph Dickson; Ordered registered.

Deed: Abraham Glisson to James Chambers for 500 acres, proved by Joseph Dickson; Ordered registered.

Deed: Shadrick Stallins to David Sloan for 150 acres, acknowledged; Ordered registered.

Deed: William Southerland to Solomon Carter for 150 acres, proved by David Greear; Ordered registered.

Deed: George Smith to John Herring for 450 acres, acknowledged; Ordered registered.

Deed: Jacob Kernegay to John Kernegay for 300 acres, proved by Wm. Dunkin; Ordered registered.

Deed: William O'Daniel to Samuel Tanner for 100 acres, proved by John Durrell; Ordered registered.

Deed: Samuel Tanner to William Whitfield for 100 acres, proved by William Whitfield; Ordered registered.

Deed: Shadrick Stallins to David Sloan for 150 acres, acknowledged; Ordered registered.

Deed: Mills Mumford to Joseph Bray, Sr., for 200 acres, proved by Samuel Houston; Ordered registered.

Deed: William Bizzel to Elisha Jernigan for 80 acres, proved by Daniel Glisson; Ordered registered.

Deed: James Pearsall, Sheriff, to Ephram Garrison for 100 acres, acknowledged; Ordered registered.

Deed: Theophilus Williams to James Morris for 4 pieces of land, acknowledged; Ordered registered.

Deed: David Cannon to John Gibbs for 85 acres, proved by Daniel Glisson; Ordered registered.

Deed: Adam Runcie to John Cox for 100 acres, proved by James Dickson; Ordered registered.

Deed: Theophilus Williams to William Whitfield for 150 acres, proved by William Dickson; Ordered registered.

George Smith, Sr., garnishee in suit of John Matchet vs. Edward Cornwallace Debruel, made oath that in his hands of said Debruels property was 2 augors, some books, some old iron & 1 kegg & no more.

Ordered John Matchet, Robert Williams, Jr. & Capt. Stephen Miller be searchers in Capt. Millers District.

Ordered the following as Jurymen to next Court: Thomas Hooks, James Wright, Cullen Conolly, Daniel Hicks, William Hooks, John Bradley, Sr., Van Wadkins, Nicholas Bowden, James Bizzell, Frederick Bearfield, John Whitehead, Sampson Grimes, James Mathews, Henry Houston, David Greer, Edward Houston, Nathan Waller, John Williams, Austin Bryan, Robert Bishop, Wm. Hollingsworth, Nicholas Hunter, Wm. Hall, Adonijah Garrison, Solomon Beesley, Wm. McGowen, Arthur Stoaks, David Murdoch, Edward Pearsall, Robert Williams, Jr., Edward Dickson, Aaron Williams, Thomas Carleton, Andrew Thally, Jesse George.

Ordered that James Gillespies Negro Warrick have liberty to carry gun on his Marsh Branch Plantation & his Negro Toney have liberty to carry gun on his home land & Plantation; Gillespie gave as securities Thomas Routledge & Charles Ward & gave bond of £50; Ordered also said Negroes be permitted to carry their guns from one Plantation to another, they keeping the direct or common path or road.

Ordered that Charles Wards Negro Friday have liberty to carry a gun on his Masters Home land & Plantation, and his Negro Roger at his Nahungah Plantation & on the direct road or path from one Plantation to the other; Ward offers as security James Gillespie & gave bond.

Ordered Tax of one shilling laid on every Poll & one shilling on every 300 acres for 1785 for contingencys of this County.

Arthur Stokes, Admin'r of Philip Rouse, dec'd, exhibited his account against estate of dec'd, amounting to £13; Allowed & Ordered filed.

Borthick Gillespie, Admin'r of Francis Lynough, dec'd, exhibited his account against estate of said dec'd, amounting to £6-7-0; Allowed & Ordered filed.

Ordered Martin Rouse, Orphan, bound apprentice to Tho. Routledge till age 21, to learn to be a Farmer & to read & write.

Ordered William Kenan, Admin'r of estate of Felix Kenan, sell perishable part of estate & report to next Court.

Court Adjourned Till Court in Course.

[signed] William Houston, Sr., Tho Routledge, Robert Dickson, Joseph Dickson, James Gillespie, Cha. Ward.

<u>16 January 1786</u> County Court Begun & Held for County of Duplin at the Court House, the 3rd Monday.

Present: Worshipfull Thomas Routledge, Charles Ward & Joseph T. Rhodes, Esquires.

Inventory of estate of Jesse Roberts, dec'd, exhibited by James Roberts, Admin'r; Ordered filed.

<u>TUESDAY MORNING</u>, Court met at 9 o'clock according to adjournment.
   Worshipfull
Present:/ Tho. Routledge, Joseph Dickson, Jospeh T. Rhodes, James Lockhart, Charles Ward, James Gillespie, Esquires.

Grand Jury sworn: William McGowen, foreman, John Whitehead, James Matthews, Nathan Waller, John Williams, Adonijah Garrison, Solomon Beesley, Edward Pearsall.

Ordered Warrin Blount, Constable, attend Grand Jury.

Additional inventory of estate of Absolom Davis, dec'd, exhibited by Moses Blackshire; Ordered filed & also Ordered filed the account current of estate of Absolom Davis, dec'd, with vouchers.

Ordered Taxes on 1,000 acres be remitted to Lewis Hines as he was charged with 1700 acres & only had 700 acres for year 1785.

Thomas Hooks took oath qualifying him as a Public Officer & a Justice of the Peace & took seat upon the Bench.

Bond from James McCulloh & And'w Bass to James McCullohs three children, Penelope, Catharin & Henry for delivery of a Negro Wench Nance, proved by William Dickson; Ordered registered.

Thomas Gray, Special Bail for Moses Branch in suit of Bryan Whitfield vs. Moses Branch, surrendered the principal to Court & was discharged; Ordered Sheriff to take Branch into custody.

Deed: Joseph Hutson to Thomas Hill for 300 acres, proved by William Dickson; Ordered registered.

Granted admin'n to James James on estate of Thomas Crossing, dec'd; James gave security & bond.

Ordered William Burton be Constable in room of John Parker the ensueing year.

Ordered that as Collector of Taxes for 1783 ought to have collected District Goal Tax of Wilmington & neglected to do so & the Collectors for that year have been compelled to account for & pay same, the Collectors be authorized to collect said Tax for 1783.

WEDNESDAY MORNING, Court met at 9 o'clock according to adjournment.

Present: Worshipfull Tho. Routledge, Charles Ward, John Beck, Sam'l Houston, Tho. Hooks, Esquires.

The Jury ordered at last Court to lay off a new road beginning at the Sampson County line at Bull Tail Branch, to lead to Duplin County Court House & join the old road near Edward Dicksons Plantation, have laid off the road as follows: beginning at the Sampson County line, running a direct course [to] cross Rockfish near Edward Dicksons Quarter, thence to Duplin Road near Bins Creek; Ordered road established, laid off & opened, William Beven, overseer with following hands to open & maintain said road: Joseph Beven, Sr., John Goff, Sr., Joseph Beven, Jr., Abraham Newton, Joshua Edwards, Elijah Bowen, Daniel Bowen, Aaron Bowen, Rubin Green, George Willis, John Alderman, Dan'l Alderman, David Alderman, Britton Powell, Hardy Powell, James Blann, Jacob Newton, James Blanton, Isaac Newton, Robert Rollins, John Little, William Blann, David Davis Joshua Blanton, John Slaughter, James Rollins, Robert Slaughter, Joseph Cartwright, David Ennis & Samuel Davis.

In suit of Charles Ward vs. Joseph Grimes, the verdict in favor of Ward, the motion for a new trial was rejected.

In suit of Joseph Grimes vs. Charles Ward, the verdict in favor of Ward, the motion for a new trial was rejected.

Deed: John Whitman to John Cranford for 141 acres, proved by Tho. Routledge; Ordered registered.

Frederick Bearfield, one of the Collector of Taxes for 1784, rendered his list of Insolvents for said year:

Alexander Laine, Sr.	£2- 3-5
Alexander Laine, Jr.	0-15-6
George Williams, Jr.	0-15-6
Thomas Gavin	0-15-6
	£4- 9-11

Ordered Frederick Bearfield allowed same in his settlement for Taxes for 1785.

Samuel Elkins, Pail for Stephen Bowen in Sasaby[?] Johnson against said Bowen, delivers Bowen to Court & is discharged.

Grand Jury released list of Orphans now in a suffering condition in the County: Elizabeth & Mary Smith living at John Carletons; William Smith living with Arthur Mathews; three Orphan children living on the NorthEast with Mrs. Summerlin nigh James Outlaws; two Mollatto children at Carters Mill belonging to Tabitha King; Jacob Smith the son of Mary Smith in service with Joseph Little, living on Rockfish; Ordered Clerk to issue citations to keepers of said Orphans to next Court.

James James, Admin'r of Thomas Crossing, dec'd, offered as securities Alex'r Dickson & Thomas Crumpton, gave Bond of £100 & took Oath of admin'r.

Inventory of estate of Thomas Crossing, dec'd, exhibited; Ordered filed.

Ordered William Hubbard overseer in room of Loftis Worley & have same hands.

Deed: Moses Hanchy to James Maxwell for 100 acres, proved by David Bunting; Ordered registered.

Deed: Hardy Revis to John Brown for 100 acres, proved by Francis Olliver; Ordered registered.

Deed: Jeremiah Chubbuck to Thomas Bennet for 63 acres, proved by John Gibbs; Ordered registered.

Deed: Ambrose Enzor to Joshua Blake for 100 acres, proved by Jacob Mathews; Ordered registered.

Deed: Henry Goodman to Steven Bearfield sundry tracts, proved by Frederick Barfield; Ordered registered.

Deed: Frederick Rivenbark to Mesheck Stallins for 100 acres, proved by Shadrick Stallins; Ordered registered.

Deed: Elijah Bowen to Mesheck Stallins for 50 acres, proved by Joseph Dickson; Ordered registered.

Deed: John Dever to Jacob Kornegay for 100 acres, proved by Steven Jones; Ordered registered.

Deed: John Vol. Taylor to Hancock Hatcher for 100 acres, proved by Daniel Hicks; Ordered registered.

Deed: James Carr to William Carr for 100 acres, proved by John Carr; Ordered registered.

Deed: Stephen Barfield to David Cannon for 420 acres, proved by William Sharples; Ordered registered.

Deed: David Cannon to William Ward for 105 acres, proved by William Sharples; Ordered registered.

Deed: Abraham Glisson to David Cannon for 200 acres, proved by Thomas James; Ordered registered.

Deed: Baker Bowden to William Taylor for 500 acres, proved by Samuel Bowden; Ordered registered.

Deed: George Smith to And'w Gufford for 75 acres, proved by James Gufford; Ordered registered.

Deed: Edward Dickson to James Dickson for 2 pieces land containing 200 acres, Acknowledged; Ordered registered.

Deed: William Moore to Felix Frederick for 2 pieces land, proved by Wm. Frederick; Ordered registered.

Deed: John Foley to Francis Olliver for 325 acres, proved by Arthur Bizzel; Ordered registered.

THURSDAY MORNING, Court met at 9 o'clock according to adjournment.

Present: Worshipfull Tho. Routledge, James Lockhart, Joseph Dickson, Robert Dickson, Charles Ward, Sam'l Houston, James Gillespie, Esquires.

Thomas Gray exhibited petition in favor of Orphans of William Stevens, dec'd, praying redress against William Stevens, Adm'r of said dec'd Estate, for their distributive share ; Ordered said William Stevens to next Court to answer petition.

Appointed Christopher Martin constable in room of Stephen Rogers.

Ordered following serve as Jurymen next Court: Lewis Thomas, John Hill, George Williams, Robert Twilley, John Williams, Caleb Quin, William Kornegay, William Grady, Stephen Gufford, Jacob Glisson, William Murphy, John Goff, Jr., David Davis, John Parker, Willis Cherry, Theoph's Williams, William Burnham, Nathan'l Kinnard, James Murray, Robert Southerland, Nathan Fountain, Henry Picket, John Waller, James Mills, James Midleton, Sr., John Mallard, James Carr, William Frederick, Daniel Glisson, James Morris, Sam'l Ward, Daniel Clarke.

Ordered John Lanier & hands of his family to clear Cypress Creek from the Bridge down to the Mouth & he & his family be exempted from working on roads the ensuing year.

Ordered Tebtha Flanagan, Orphan about 9, Bound to James Midleton, Jr. for & during the term of 8 years from this date to learn to read the Bible & to weave, etc.; Midleton offers as Securities Robert Dickson & Arthur Stoakes & gave Bond of £100.

Allowed Warrin Blount 24 shillings for attending Court as constable 3 days.

Alexander Lanier offered as security against Estate of Henry Eustice McCulloh £169-6-8 & £3-10-11 costs & as also there was another judgement obtained by Joseph Herring against William Kenan, Adm'r of Felix Kenan, dec'd, for £71-6-8 & also £2-13-9 costs, for which judgement Court granted so much property of McCulloh be retained by William Kenan to satisfy said Judgement & costs, therefore Ordered Clerk issue summons against all persons indebted to said McCulloh to appear next Court to ahow cause why execution of said judgement should not issue against said garnishee for property in their hands.

Thomas Routledge, Gaurdian to Martin Rouse, Orphan of Philip Rouse, dec'd, Exhibited petition in favor of said Orphan against Arthur Stokes, Adm'r of Philip Rouse, dec'd; Ordered Arthur Stokes summoned to next Court to answer petition.

Allowed William Magee 16 shillings for attending Court as constable 2 days.

FRIDAY MORNING. Court met at 9 o'clock according to adjournment.

Present: Worshipfull Tho. Routledge, Charles Ward, Joseph Dickson, James Gillespie, Esquires.

Charles Ward is continued as Coroner; he gave Bond of £1,000.

Act of General Assembly at Newbern 1784 directed the County Courts to appoint a person in each Captains District to take list of number of White & Black Inhabitants & the free Citizens of every age, sex & condition in each District, which list shall distinguish Blacks from Whites & other free Inhabitants;

Court appoints as follows:
For Capt. Gillespies Co. - Thomas Routledge
For Capt. Millers Co. - Charles Ward
For Capt. Kenans Co. - Daniel Hicks
For Capt. Southerlands Co. - Robert Southerland
For Capt. Stallins Co. - Daniel Teachy
For Capt. Hubbards Co. - Samuel Houston
For Capt. Bowdens Co. - Francis Olliver
For Capt. Whiteheads Co. - Frederick Bearfield

As the Bridge over the NorthEast River at Mouth of Limestone Creek is not properly finished according to Law, Ordered William Hall have said Bridge finished immediately & that Joseph Thomas Rhodes, Robt. Southerland & William McGowen be a Committee to inspect Bridge & report to next Court.

Ordered William Hall summoned to next Court to answer such objections as may be suggested against him by Court for charging & receiving other or greater toll than allowed & also for charging toll for persons crossing before Bridge is finished & that he be prepared to give Bond; Ordered William Magee to serve notice on him.

Allowed William Dickson, Clerk of Court, £15 for extra services for 1785.

Additional account against Estate of Francis Lynough, dec'd, Exhibited by Borthrik Gillespie, Adm'r, amounting to £4-18-0; Ordered filed.

James Gillespie offered himself responsible for Borthrik Gillespies adm'n of Estate of Francis Lynough, dec'd.

Ordered Peter Young to bring to next Court Eulee Lynough, Orphan of Francis Lynough, dec'd, to chuse her guardian.

Court Adjourned Till Court in Course.

[signed]   Tho. Routledge, Joseph Dickson, Cha. Ward,
           James Gillespie.

17 APRIL 1786
County Court Begun & Held for County of Duplin at the Court House, the 3rd Monday.

Present: Worshipfull Thomas Routledge, Joseph Dickson, Kedar Bryan, Esquires.

In suit of State vs. Rich Meares, defendant came before Court, submitted & fined 6 pence & costs.

Ordered Thomas Johnston be Overseer of Road in room of James Midleton & have same hands.

TUESDAY MORNING, Court met at 9 o'clock according to adjournment.

Present: Worshipfull Thomas Routledge, Joseph Dickson, Kedar Bryan, Esquires.

Ordered Jacob Smith, Orphan about 7 years of age, Bound an Apprentice to Nathaniel Waller till he be 21, to learn to read & write & trade of House Carpenter.

Ordered Sarah Bruington, Orphan age 3, Bound Apprentice to Jacob Wells till age 18, to learn to read the Bible & to spin & weave.

Grand Jury sworn: Lewis Thomas, foreman, Rob Southerland, George Williams, William Frederick, John Hill, James Midleton, Sr., Caleb Quin, William Kornegay, Stephen Gufford, Jacob Glisson, William Murphy, John Goff, Jr., John Mallard, James Carr, Robert Twilly, Theophilus Williams, Willis Cherry.

Ordered Warrin Blount, Constable, attend Grand Jury.

Thomas Gray, Ex'r of Alex'r Gray, dec'd, vs. Abe Jones, defendant surrendered himself to Court in discharge of his bail; Ordered said Bail discharged & said Jones taken into Sheriffs custody.

In suit of Nathan Waller vs. Abe Jones, defendant surrendered himself to Court in discharge of his bail; Ordered said Bail discharged & said Jones taken into Sheriffs custody.

Appointed Mildred Stevens Guardian to her daughter Eulee Stevens, Orphan of William Stevens, dec'd; she gave Bond of £600 & offered as securities Thomas Gray & John Beck.

Francis Olliver returned his list of number of White & Black persons given in in his District; Ordered filed.

Solomon Picket, charged with 640 acres Tax in 1785, appears to have been a mistake; Ordered Picket dischraged from paying same.

Appointed John Farrior Overseer of Road in room of William Hollingsworth.

Ordered James Rivers [?], Orphan Mulatto one year of age the 16 July 1785, Bound Apprentice to Abraham Molten, Jr. till age 21, to learn to read & write & the trade of a Cordwainer; Molten offers as Securities James Kenan & Joseph Dickson & gave Bond of £500.

Elizabeth Lockhart, Widow of James Lockhart, dec'd, granted Adm'n on Estate of her dec'd husband, offers as securities Anthony Miller & Samuel Houston & gave Bond of £500.

Daniel Hicks returned his list of White & Black persons in his District; Ordered filed.

Barnabas Stevens & Douglas Powell, summoned as garnishees of McCulloh in suit of Joseph Herring vs. Kenan, Adm'r on account of McCulloh, appeared; Ordered discharged; In suit of same vs. same James Sampson & Richard Clinton summoned as garnishees; Ordered discharged; In suit of same vs. same John Buck, Sampson Young, Stephen Blackman & Arthur Dobbs Young, summoned as garnishees; Ordered discharged.

Ordered Joseph Williams,Jr. be Overseer in room of Fred'k Wells.

In suit of Arthur Stokes, Adm'r of Philip Rouse, vs. William Allen, Ezeck'l Allen & Henry Jones; John Cook, special bail, surrendered Ezekiel Allen & Henry Jones to Court & was discharged; Ordered Sheriff to take them into custody.

WEDNESDAY MORNING, Court met at 9 o'clock according to adjournment.

Present: Worshipfull John Beck, Joseph T.Rhodes, James Outlaw, Kedar Bryan, Dan'l Teachy & Thomas Hooks, Esquires.

Charles Ward returned his list of White & Black Inhabitants; Ordered filed.

Robin Southerland returned his list of White & Black Inhabitants; Ordered filed.

James McCulloh, summoned as garnishee to Henry Eustice McCulloh, dec'd, swore he entered into Bond with Samuel Ward & Stephen Herring to Felix Kenan, agent to said Henry E. McCulloh on the 21st day of August, 1777 in the penalty of £200, conditioned for the payment of £50 on 25th December, 1779 payable to said Henry E.McCulloh & the Garnishee further states that Samuel Ward & Stephen Herring were his securities; he also says that he singly entered into Bond in penalty of £200 conditioned for payment of £100 with lawful interest to said Henry E.McCulloh payable 13 February, 1775; Garnishee further says that an Annuity of £30 was settled upon him by Henry E.McCulloh about 1775 which is on record in Duplin Co. Court & of this Annuity the Garnishee received only 2 or 3 years & the other years are yet oweing; the years paid were discharged by Felix Kenan, agent to said McCulloh & for Bond of first date 1777, Henry E.McCulloh acknowledged satisfaction & the arrears due on aforesaid Annuity are more than equal to the discharge of the other Bond.

Joseph T.Rhodes, Daniel Southerland & William McGowen, a Committee to Inspect the Bridge across the NorthEast River at Limestone, reported in writing that the Bridge is unfinished & dangerous to pass over.

Ordered Daniel Glisson be Constable in room of Warrin Blount & also in room of Elisha Jernigan in each of their Districts.

Ordered John Duff be Constable in room of Rice Mathews.

Sam'l Houston returned his list of White & Black persons; Ordered filed.

Daniel Teachy returned his list of White & Black persons; Ordered filed.

Joseph Johnston summoned as garnishee to Henry Eustice McCulloh swore he owes McCulloh £11-7-0, the balance of principal due on his Bond & the interest, no more.

Ordered Wm. Taylor exempted from payment of Taxes for his Negro wench Ann, she being infirm & useless to her Master.

THURSDAY MORNING, Court met at 9 o'clock according to adjournment.

Present: Worshipfull William Houston, William Taylor, Thomas Hooks, Thomas Routledge, Kedar Bryan, Joseph Dickson, Esquires.

Silvia Williams charged Snodon Pearse with begeting her Bastard Child, now upwards of 2 years old, & she has never received anything from said Pearse toward maintenance of child; Ordered Pearse shall pay to Silvia Williams £12 for maintaining said Child for past 2 years & also 30 shillings to maintain Child till next Court.

Thomas Routledge returned his list of White & Black inhabitants; Ordered filed.

Granted Joseph Grimes petition to build a Public Grist Mill over Cypress Creek where he has land on one side of the Creek & the land on the other side is known as Cockers land; Ordered petition filed.

Ordered Buckner Killigrew & Owen O'Daniel be Searchers in District of Capt. Whiteheads Co.

Frederick Bearfield returned his list of White & Black persons; Ordered filed.

Deed: Samuel Ashe, Jr. to Jacob Boney for 400 acres, proved by Shadrick Stallins; Ordered registered.

Deed: William Stevens to William Hurst for 324 acres, proved by John Beck; Ordered registered.

Deed: John Whitehead to John Winders for 3 pieces land, proved by James Grimes; Ordered registered.

Deed: William Merritt to Frederick Smith for 50 acres, Acknowledged; Ordered registered.

Deed: Joseph Grimes to Sampson Grimes [no amount of land], Acknowledged; Ordered registered.

Deed: John Cook to William Knight for 50 acres, proved by Jacob Matthews; Ordered registered.

Deed: William Kenan to Jesse Brown for 100 acres, Acknowledged; Ordered registered.

Deed: Thomas Burton to James Evens for 400 acres, Acknowledged; Ordered registered.

Deed: Theophilus Williams to [no first name] Cook for 100 acres, Acknowledged; Ordered registered.

Deed: Samuel Albertson & John Albertson to Windell Davis for 2 tracts land, proved by Michael Glisson; Ordered registered.

Deed: William Boyet to Lewis Thomas for 400 acres, proved by James Kenan; Ordered registered.

Deed: Joseph Dickson to Lewis Thomas for 330 acres, Acknowledged; Ordered registered.

In suit of Eliza Fussell vs. Duff & Bowen, caveat & suspension at April Term 1785, the Jury being convened on the premises & verdict for Elijah Bowen, verdict for Elizabeth Fussell in part; Ordered Clerk issue transcript of verdict certified to the Secretary for Mrs. Fussell.

Ordered Jesse George & Jacob Boney be Searchers or Patrolers in District of Capt. Stallings Co.

Ordered Commission issued to John James in New Hanover Co. to take examination of Isabel Johns, wife of John Johns, concerning execution of 2 Deeds from said John Johns & Isabel Johns to James James in Duplin Co. & transmit same to next Court.

Ordered Clerk of this Court to issue scitation to Coroner of Dobbs Co. to notice Robert White, Sheriff of Dobbs Co., to appear before Duplin Co. Court the 3rd Monday in July next to answer to said Court for returning sundry executions against Adm'rs of Daniel Waite & not returning any money therein.

Ordered John Johnston of Burncoat, Overseer of Road & NorthEast River in room of Samuel Sowell & have same hands.

Ordered Stephen Gufford be Constable in room of Richard Mouns [?] .

Ordered John Hill & William Kenan work on Road leading from Bear Swamp at Thomas Hooks down to Nahunga Swamp, under Thomas Hooks, Overseer.

Whereas Road Ordered to be laid off from Bulltail on Rockfish to join Duplin Road near Edward Dicksons, is found to be disagreeable & inconvenient to a great number of the Inhabitants, Ordered said road discontinued.

Ordered Old Road leading from Goshen at John Hills to Stewarts Creek be discontinued.

Ordered Joseph Thomas Rhodes, Samuel Houston, Joseph Grimes & James Morris be Jurors to Wilmington Superior Court the 6th June next.

Ordered Francis Olliver, Nicholas Bowden, Elisha Jernigan, Samuel Rogers, Frederick Bearfield, Michael Glisson, William Guy, Felix Frederick, James Wright, John Clarke, Nicholas Hunter, James McIntire, Alexander Dickson, Phil. Southerland, William Rigby, James Midleton (Miller), Stephen Miller, Edward Pearsall, John Matchet, Ivey Smith, Jacob Boney, Frederick Williams, Joseph Williams,Jr., Andrew Thally, Daniel Southerland, John Williams, Jr., Auston Bryan, Henry Newkirk, George Smith, Jr., Edward Houston & William Hubbard as Jurors to Next Court.

Deed: Joab Padgett to Isaac Hunter for 212 acres, proved by Arthur Stokes; Ordered registered.

Granted Edward Houston a licence to keep a Tavern at his own house in this County, he offered as Securities William Houston & William Hubbard & gave Bond.

The several Collectors of General Taxes in this County have satisfied this Court that it is not in their power to settle & make their returns to this Court & get the allowance of Insolvents completed in order to settle with the County Treasurer before he must settle with the State Treasurer; Ordered that Thom's Routledge, Robert Dickson, Charles Ward & Joseph Dickson, they or any three, settle with said Collectors & allow such Insolvents as may ne proved to their satisfaction, which allowances shall be attested by the Clerk as if made in Court & shall be good in their settlement with the Sheriff.

The Commissioners of the uper District of Goshen made report on clearing the main run of Goshen; Ordered William Beck & his Company work this season from the Bluff above the Mouth of Panther down to a Bent of run opposite a point of land that extends into the swamp opposite William Dicksons Plantation.

Ordered Hillary Hooks & his Company work this season from Bent of run at lower end of William Becks District down to where the two runs meet a little below the Bridge.

Ordered John Bradley & his Company work this season from the main landing place at the Bridge down to Samuel Wards little slew.

Ordered Willis Cherry & his Company to work this season from uper end of Samuel Wards slew down to uper end of Cannons slew.

Ordered Daniel Glisson & his Company to work this season the same District as last year.

Ordered that the said Overseers work under the immediate direction of Commissioners appointed over the uper division of the Swamp, that if any Overseer shall die, refuse to act or remove, the Commissioners, or any two, shall appoint a proper person to act in his stead until the Court shall appoint another.

Commissioners for the middle District of Goshen made their report; Ordered that the Districts as laid off last year in that division of the Swamp shall stand & remain without any alteration this year & the several Overseers & their Companies shall remain without any alteration except that John Ward shall be Overseer in room of Theophilus Williams.

Commissioners of the lower division of Goshen Swamp made their report; appointed John Matchet Commissioner in room of & instead of Daniel Herring who is removed; Ordered Stephen Miller Overseer of all hands that were in his own District & in John Matchets District last year & that his District shall include all the run that belonged to him & John Matchet last year.

Ordered Owen O'Daniel Overseer in room of Stephen Herring & have same hands & District.

Ordered Uriah Gurganus Overseer in room of Joseph Grimes & have same hands & District.

Ordered David Cannon continued as Overseer & have same hands & District as last year.

Ordered Sampson Grimes continued as Overseer & have same hands & District as last year.

Court Adjourned Till Court in Course.

[signed]   Wm.Houston,Sr., Tho. Routledge, Kedar Bryan,
           Joseph Dickson.

June 3, 1786, Duplin County

In Pursuance of an Order of Court past, last April Term, Appointing Tho's Routledge, Robert Dickson, Charles Ward & Joseph Dickson a Court to settle with the Collectors of Taxes in this County for 1785 & to allow them such Insolvents as to them might seem just, the said Court proceeded & allowed as follows:

To Thomas Wright, Collector

Persons Insolvent	Polls	Acres	Gen'l Tax	County Tax	Poor Tax	Court House Tax	Goal Tax	Continental Tax
Josiah Benton	1		0-12-0	0-1-0	0-1-0	0-1-0	0-0-6	0-1-6
Hardy Benton, Sr.	1		12-0	1-0	1-0	1-0	-6	1-6
Hardy Benton, Jr.	1	100	16-0	1-4	1-4	1-4	-8	2-0
Samuel Benton	1	100	16-0	1-4	1-4	1-4	-8	2-0
John Rogers	1		12-0	1-0	1-0	1-0	-6	1-6
Solomon Singar	1		12-0	1-0	1-0	1-0	-6	1-6
James Moore	1	98	16-0	1-4	1-4	1-4	-8	2-0
George Outlaw	1	125	17-0	1-7	1-7	1-7	-10	2-4
James Goodman	2	420	2-10-10	3-5	3-5	3-5	1-9	5-0
			£7-13-10	13/	13/	13/	6/7	19/4

To William Wells, Collector

Persons Insolvent	Polls	Acres	Gen'l Tax	County Tax	Poor Tax	Court House Tax	Goal Tax	Continental Tax
John Butler	1		0-12-0	0-1-0	0-1-0	0-1-0	0-0-6	0-1-6
Claudius Cartright	1	300	1- 4-0	2-0	2-0	2-0	1-0	3-0
Rubin Green	1	100	16-0	1-4	1-4	1-4	-8	2-0
Joshua Lee	1		12-0	1-0	1-0	1-0	-6	1-6
Sarah Newton		100	4-0	0-4	0-4	0-4	-2	-6
Andrew Neeley	1	200	1-0-0	1-8	1-8	1-8	-10	2-6
George Gooding	1		12-0	1-0	1-0	1-0	-6	1-6
David Alpin	1		12-0	1-0	1-0	1-0	-6	1-6
Nicholas Fennel	1		12-0	1-0	1-0	1-0	-6	1-6
Job Smith	1	600	1-16-0	3-0	3-0	3-0	1-6	4-6
Elijah Waller	1	200	1-0- 0	1-8	1-8	1-8	-10	2-6
Samuel Carman	1		12-0	1-0	1-0	1-0	-6	1-6
Zeb Hollingsworth	1		12-0	1-0	1-0	1-0	-6	1-6
Stephen Parish	1		12-0	1-0	1-0	1-0	-6	1-6
Archibald Pearse	1	350	1-6- 0	2-2	2-2	2-2	1-1	3-3
Snodon Pearse	1		12-0	1-0	1-0	1-0	-6	1-6
James Williams	1	790	2- 3-7	3-7	3-7	3-7	1-9	5-6
Thomas Crossing	1		12-0	1-0	1-0	1-0	-6	1-6

[to William Wells, continued]

Persons Insolvent	Polls	Acres	Gen'l Tax	County Tax	Poor Tax	Court House Tax	Goal Tax	Continental Tax
David Williams	1		0-12-0	0-1-0	0-1-0	0-1-0	0-0-6	0-1-6
Henry Jones	1	100	16-0	1-4	1-4	1-4	0-8	2-0
Samuel Sandlin (18/8 paid in certificate)	1	340	13-8	3-2	3-2	3-2	1-6	4-6
Deduction for mistake in Clks		1,850						
Deduction for J's Pucket		640						
			£18-18-5	1-15-4	1-15-4	1-15-4	18-8	2-13-0

Ordered the above lists filed & Clerk certifie above allowances to Sheriff & Public Treasurer.

[signed] Tho. Routledge, Joseph Dickson, Robert Dickson.

Frederick Barfield rendered his list of Insolvents & was allowed as follows:

Persons Insolvent	Polls	Acres	Gen'l Tax	County Tax	Poor Tax	Court House Tax	Goal Tax	Continental Tax
John Brock	1	200	1-0-0	0-1-8	0-1-8	0-1-8	0-0-11	0-2-6
Samuel Powers	1	200	1-0-0	1-8	1-8	1-8	-11	2-6
William Sulliven	1	1,715	4-0-9	6-9	6-9	6-9	3-5	10-3
John Smith	1	100	16-0	1-4	1-4	1-4	0-8	2-0
Lemon Dunn	2		1-4-0	2-0	2-0	2-0	1-0	3-0
Jonathan Taylor	1		12-0	1-0	1-0	1-0	-6	1-6
Flud Foley	1		12-0	1-0	1-0	1-0	-6	1-6
Mathew Ganey	1		12-0	1-0	1-0	1-0	-6	1-6
Stephen Tilman	2		1-4-0	2-0	2-0	2-0	1-0	3-0
Peter Hall	1		12-0	1-0	1-0	1-0	-6	1-6

[Frederick Barfield, continued]

Persons Insolvent	Polls	Acres	Gen'l Tax	County Tax	Poor Tax	Court House Tax	Goal Tax	Continental Tax
Samson Jones	1		0-12-0	0-1-0	0-1-0	0-1-0	0-0-6	0-1-6
Thomas Welch	1		12-0	1-0	1-0	1-0	-6	1-6
			£12-16-9	1-1-5	1-1-5	1-1-5	10-9	1-12-2

Ordered above list filed & Clerk certifie above allowances to Sheriff & Public Treasurer.

[signed] Tho. Routledge, Joseph Dickson, Robert Dickson.

17 July 1786
County Court Begun & Held for County of Duplin, the 3rd Monday.

Present: Worshipfull W. Houston, Tho. Routledge, Robert Dickson, John Beck, James Gillespie, Esquires.

Ordered Betsey Smith & Celia Smith, two Orphan children, Betsey about 10 years of age & Celia about 5, Bound Apprentices to John Carleton till age 18 or be married & to learn to read the Bible & write & other qualifications fit for women.

Ordered William Smith, Orphan, Bound Apprentice to William Goff till age 21, he being now 14, to learn the trade of Wheel Wright & to read & write etc.

Ordered William Southerland, Constable, to forthwith bring before the Court Anna Henderson & her four children that they may be dealt with all as law directs.

Granted John Hills petition for his Negro Cesar to carry a gun on his own land, he offered for Security James Kenan & gave Bond of £50.

Ordered Stephen Miller to deliver up to John Hill the gun he took from his Negro Cesar.

TUESDAY MORNING, Court met at 9 o'clock according to adjournment.

Present: Worshipfull Thomas Routledge, Joseph Dickson, John Beck, Samuel Houston, Kedar Bryan.

Suckey Newton, a single woman, charged Luke Ward, Jr. with begeting her Bastard Child; Court adjudged that said Luke Ward shall pay said Suckey Newton 10 shillings for each & every month from birth of child till this time & that Suckey

Newton shall keep & maintain said child 12 months more from this time & that Luke Ward shall pay her 10 shillings for each month at the expiration of said Term.

List of Sales of Estate of Thomas Crossing, dec'd, exhibited; Ordered filed.

Grand Jury sworn: Francis Olliver, foreman, Samuel Rogers, Michael Glisson, Felix Frederick, James Wright, Nicholas Hunter, William Rigbee, Edward Pearsall, John Matchet, Andrew Thally, Daniel Southerland, Edward Houston, Elisha Jernigan, Henry Newkirk.

Ordered William Magee, Constable, to attend Grand Jury.

John Woodward convened before the Court for contempt of authority in rescueing a certain Public Mare which he had detained & which was taken from him by William Southerland, a Constable, by legal warrant from under the hand of a Justice of the Peace; Ordered John Woodward committed to Goal for said contempt & rescue.

William Wells, one of the Collectors of Taxes for 1785, rendered his list of supernumerys, collected by him, amounting to £10-19-0 General Tax, 19/4 County Tax, 19/4 Court House Tax, 19/4 Parish Tax, 9/8 District Goal Tax, £1-9-0 Continental Tax; Ordered filed & said William Wells pay said Public & other Taxes to Clerk of this Court where it is to remain till otherwise ordered by Court.

Inventory of Estate of James Lockhart, dec'd, Exhibited by the Adm'r; Ordered filed.

William Taylor took Oath for qualification of Public Officers & Oath of a Justice of the Peace & took his seat upon the Bench.

Granted James James leave to erect a House or Barr for the purpose of selling victuals & Drink in Public times upon the Court House Lot, the place whereto erect said House to be shewed him by Court or a Committee of the Court.

Court proceeded to the Election of a Sheriff; present on the Bench were the Worshipfull William Houston, Tho. Routledge, Robert Dickson, William Taylor, Joseph Dickson, Charles Ward, Samuel Houston, John Beck, James Gillespie, Kedar Bryan, James Outlaw, Daniel Teachy, Joseph T. Rhodes, Thomas Hooks, & elected the Honorable James Kenan, Esquire to the Office of Sheriff & Ordered Clerk to certifie same.

Ordered Capt. William Taylors two hands & Jesse Swinson to work on Goshen under Lavin Watkins, Overseer.

Granted petition of sundry Inhabitants of uper part of the
County on the NorthEast & North side of Goshen Swamp to have
a Public Road laid off from lower Grove Bridge to cross Goshen
Swamp at or near Charles Wards Plantation & from thence to the
NorthEast at or near John Kornegays Plantation & from thence
to the Bounds of the County nearly opposite William Reeves in
Waine County; Ordered Frederick Barfield, John Winders,Jr.,
George Kornegay, William Dunkin, Rubin Johnston, John Kornegay,
Edmund Dunkin, Jr., Sam'l Bowden, James Grimes, Joseph Smith,
Archibald Carr, Edward Pearsall, Jesse Brock, Anthony Jones
& Adam Reeves, they or any 12 be a Jury to lay off said Road
& report a Plan thereof to the next Court.

Ordered Edmund Dunkin,Jr. summon & convene said Jury at
Charles Wards Plantation on a convenient time to proceed to
lay off said Road & Charles Ward to Qualify said Jury.

Ordered Edmund Dunkin,Jr. be Constable in District of Capt.
Bowdens Company.

WEDNESDAY MORNING, Court met at 9 o'clock according to
adjournment.

Present: Worshipfull William Houston, Tho. Routledge, Robert
Dickson, Joseph Dickson, William Taylor, Charles Ward, James
Gillespie, Kedar Bryan, Thomas Hooks, Samuel Houston, John
Beck, Daniel Teachy, Esquires.

Martha Maning, a single woman, charged Richard Bradley with
begeting her Bastard Child which is $2\frac{1}{2}$ years of age the
28th day of this Inst. July; Ordered said Bradley pay Martha
Maning 10 shillings for each month from Childs birth to this
date & Martha Maning shall keep & maintain Child for 12 months
from this date & be allowed 10 shillings for each month
which Richard Bradley shall pay her.

THURSDAY MORNING, Court met at 9 o'clock according to
adjournment.

Present: Worshipfull William Houston, Tho. Routledge, Robert
Dickson, Joseph Dickson, William Taylor, James Gillespie,
Kedar Bryan, Joseph T.Rhodes, Daniel Teachy, Thomas Hooks,
Esquires.

Ordered Asa Chance, Orphan age 14, living with John Houseman
be delivered by Houseman to Edmond Dunkin & by said Dunkin
be brought to next Court.

Ordered Mary Ann Creamer, a Mullatto one year old the 15th
of last April, Bound Apprentice to Sarah Routledge till age
21 to learn to read & write, etc.; she offers for Securities

Thomas Routledge & Robert Dickson & gave Bond of £200 for good usuage of said Orphan

Ordered Isabel Allen, Widow, be noticed to bring to next Court her three children, John, Peggy & Nancy.

Ordered Widow Jones, on NorthEast, scited to bring her son, Lewis Jones, to next Court to be dealt with as Law directs.

The Jury being sworn in the suit of Abigal Brice vs. Daniel Southerland & being sent out dispersed without returning & giving any Verdict & upon being called ten only appeared.

Ordered Jonathan Kitley be Searcher in Capt. Whiteheads Company instead of Buckner Killigrew.

Ordered James Gillespie, Joseph Dickson, Kedar Bryan be a Committee to settle the Estate of Philip Rouse, dec'd, with Arthur Stokes, Adm'r & report to next Court.

~~Ordered Abraham Newkirk be Overseer of Road in room of John Magee.~~

Thomas Gray, Esquire, appointed Soliciter for the State in this County.

Hon'l James Kenan, Esquire, produced a Commission from the Governor appointing him Sheriff of this County, he gave Bond of £5,000 for execution of his office as Sheriff & £10,000 for execution of his office as County Treasurer & took Oath of Office as Sheriff.

FRIDAY MORNING, Court met at 9 o'clock according to adjournment.

Present: Worshipfull William Houston, Tho. Routledge, James Gillespie & Samuel Houston, Esquires.

Deed: Aaron Williams to Jacob Wells for 100 acres, proved by Adam Platt; Ordered registered.

Deed: Aaron Williams to Adam Platt for 100 acres, proved by Jacob Wells; Ordered registered.

Deed: Tho's Wiggins to George Homes for 100 acres, Acknowledged; Ordered registered.

Deed: John Woodward to Elisha Woodward for 320 acres, Acknowledged; Ordered registered.

Deed: John B. Sheppard to Rob't Williams for 100 acres, proved by Benja. Best; Ordered registered.

Deed: Arthur Stokes to John Mallard for 2 pieces land, proved by Phil Southerland; Ordered registered.

Deed: Abraham Newkirk to Henry Newkirk for 100 acres, Acknowledged; Ordered registered.

Deed: Richard Singleton to Fred'k Wells for 100 acres, Acknowledged; Ordered registered.

Deed: James Love to John B. Sheppard for 100 acres, proved by Joseph Dickson; Ordered registered.

Deed: John Rivenbark to Dan'l Boney for 100 acres, proved by Dan'l Teachy; Ordered registered.

Deed: John Beck to William Beck for 85 acres, Acknowledged; Ordered registered.

Deed: John Beck to Stephen Beck for 278 acres, Acknowledged; Ordered registered.

Deed: James Ellis to Benja. Lanier for 100 acres, proved by John Lanier; Ordered registered.

Deed: Henry Allen to James Hall for 50 acres, Acknowledged; Ordered registered.

Deed: James McIntire to John Mallard for 100 acres, proved by Phil Southerland; Ordered registered.

Deed: Frederick Wells to Aaron Williams for 15 acres, proved by Shadrick Stallins; Ordered registered.

Deed: William Houston & Edward Houston to the Commissioners of Soracta for sundry Lotts, Acknowledged; Ordered registered.

Ordered Edward Houston be Overseer of River in room of Samuel Houston & that Joseph Morgan, William Nebucut & Frederick Grady be added to said District.

Allowed William Dickson 12 shillings for a Book he purchased for a Court Action Docket.

Ordered a Tax of one shilling on every Poll Taxable Person & 4 pence on every 100 acres & on Town Lotts in proportion for discharging contingencies of County for 1786.

Ordered Frederick Barfield, William Graddy, Sr., Anthony Jones, Stephen Barfield, William Taylor, Jr., Stephen Snell, John Haines, Thomas Flowers, William Stevens, John Clark, Patrick Newton, Thomas Hill, William Kenan, Charles Brown, Joseph Smith, John Williams (B.C.), Sam'l Sowell, William Nethercut, Sr., Robert Twilley, Wm. Hollingsworth, Richard Williams, Drury Hall, Nathan Fountain, Robert Sloan, David Sloan, Jacob Wells, Jr., Fred'k Wells, John Molten, James McIntire, William Stokes, Benjamin Tanner & William Carr be Jury Men for next Court.

Ordered William Southerland & Daniel Glisson be Inspectors of the Poll at ensueing election.

Ordered Joseph Thomas Rhodes take list of Taxables in District of Capt. Southerlands Company.

Ordered Samuel Houston take list of Taxables for Capt. Hubbards Company.

Ordered James Outlaw take list of Taxables for District of Capt. Whiteheads Company.

Ordered William Taylor take list of Taxables for District of Capt. Bowdens Company.

Ordered Kedar Bryan take list of Taxables for District of Capt. Kenans Company.

Ordered Daniel Teachy to take list of Taxables for District of Capt. Stallins Company.

Ordered Joseph Dickson take list of Taxables for District of Capt. Gillespies Company.

Ordered Charles Ward take list of Taxables for District of Capt. Millers Company.

Ordered the several constables in each District or Captains Company shall summon Inhabitants of their Districts to give in their Taxable property to the Justices appointed to take same, in due time.

Granted James James license to keep a Tavern at his House & he offered as Securities Stephen Miller & William Magee & gave Bond.

Ordered Sarah Henderson, Orphan about 12 years old last March, Bound Apprentice to John Natchet till age 18 to learn to read & write.

Ordered James Henderson, Orphan about 8 years old the 19th August last year, now almost 9, Bound Apprentice to James Pearsall till age 21, to learn to read & write & trade of a Shoe Maker.

Ordered Lucy Henderson, Orphan Mullatto age 3 last March, Bound Apprentice to William Southerland till age 21 & to learn to read & write, etc. Also Ordered William Southerland give Bond of £300 for good usuage of said child & he will not remove her out of said State, he offers as securities Robert Dickson & James Gillespie.

Ordered Daniel Southerland be Overseer of Road in room of John Magee & have same hands.

Allowed William Magee 32 shillings for attending Court as constable 4 days this Court.

Allowed William Magee 24 shillings for attending Court as constable 3 days last April.

Allowed Daniel Glisson 24 shillings for attending Court as constable 3 days this Court.

Ordered Robert Dickson be continued as Commissioner of NorthEast River as formerly.

Ordered Samuel Houston be Commissioner of River in room of Joseph Tho. Rhodes.

Ordered William McGowen be Commissioner of River in room of James Gillespie.

Ordered Prison Bounds be laid off for the bebefit of Prisoners & the Court have also laid off as follows: including the whole Bounds of the Court House Lott & James Pearsalls House & Common Yard & Spring & the open Common Way between the said Lott & Pearsalls Spring & House.

Ordered James Pearsall have leave to build a house on Court House Lott for purpose of selling victuals & liquors in Public Times, which House he shall build on the Out edge of said Lott as farr remote from Court House as convenience will admit.

Granted John Moltens petition for his Negro Bob to carry a gun & hunt on his own land; he offered as Security James James & James Pearsall & gave Bond.

Ordered Alexander Dickson, William McGowen & James Carr be Searchers for Capt. Gillespies Company.

Ordered Jonathan Kitley scited to appear next Court to show cause why he may not be discontinued from being Searcher in Capt. Whiteheads Company .

Court Adjourned Till Court in Course.

[signed] Wm. Houston, Sr., Tho. Routledge, Robert Dickson, Sam'l Houston, James Gillespie.

16 October 1786, County Court Begun & Held for County of Duplin at the Court House, the 3rd Monday.

Present: Worshipfull Thomas Routledge, Esquire.

There appearing no other Justice to hold this Court, it is Ordered the Court be adjourned till tommorrow morning at 9 o'clock.

TUESDAY MORNING, Court met at 9 o'clock according to adjournment.

Present: Worshipfull Thomas Routledge, Robert Dickson, Charles Ward, Samuel Houston, James Gillespie, Esquires.

Deed: James Lockhart to Lincoln Shuffield for 130 acres, proved by Joseph Dickson; Ordered registered.

Deed: John Merchant to Adonijah Garrison for 100 acres, proved by Robert Dickson; Ordered registered.

Deed: Wimbert Boney to Adonijah Garrison for 20 acres, proved by Robert Dickson; Ordered registered.

Deed: Robert Dickson to Alexander Dickson for 50 acres, Acknowledged; Ordered registered.

Deed: Alexander Dickson to Robert Dickson for 50 acres, proved by James Dickson; Ordered registered.

Deed: James Pearsall to Robert Dickson for 80 acres, Acknowledged; Ordered registered.

Deed: Robert & William Dickson to Robert Dickson for 250 acres, Acknowledged; Ordered registered.

Deed: William & Robert Dickson to William Dickson for 540 acres, Acknowledged; Ordered registered.

Deed: John Wright to his son Thomas Wright for 2 pieces land, 400 acres, proved by William Dickson; Ordered registered.

Deed: George Smith to Robert Ivey for 150 acres, proved by Josiah Stafford; Ordered registered.

Ordered Nathaniel Wells, aged & having no property, be exempted from being Taxed as a Poll Taxable person.

Deed: George Willis to Ambrose Enzor for 150 acres, proved by Elijah Bowen; Ordered registered.

Ordered James Gillespie, Executor of John James E. Augustus Carter, dec'd, sell at Publick under a certian specie certificate of ₤28-5-4 for ready money to discharge the debts due by said Estate as there appears to be no other property in his hands.

Account of sales of Estate of James Lockhart, dec'd, Exhibited by Sheriff; Ordered filed.

Jury summoned & William Grady, Sr., Anth'y Jones, Stephen Barfield, John Harris, Tho. Flowers, William Kenan, John Williams (Burncoat), Sam'l Sowell, William Nethercut, Jr., Richard Williams, Fred'k Well's & Wm. Carr failing to answer; Ordered they be fined & scited to appear at next Court to show cause why they shall not be ? agreeable to Act of Assembly.

Deed: Joseph Williams to his son David Williams for 150 acres, Acknowledged; Ordered registered.

Deed: Lois Newton & Abraham Newton to John Little for 85 acres, proved by Aaron Williams; Ordered registered.

Deed: Lois Newton & Abraham Newton to John Little for 100 acres, proved by Aaron Williams; Ordered registered.

Deed: Charles Merrit to Benjamin Ezel for 50 acres, Acknowledged; Ordered registered.

Deed: William Wilkins to Lewis Hines for 200 acres, proved by Isaac Hines; Ordered registered.

Deed: Samuel Tanner to Jesse Pipkin for 60 acres, proved by Isaac Hines; Ordered registered.

Deed: George Cooper, Sr. to George Cooper, Jr. for 97 acres, Acknowledged; Ordered registered.

Deed: [no first name] Jones to John Weedens for 200 acres, proved by William Nethercut; Ordered registered.

Deed: James Pearsall, Sheriff, to John Boney for 200 acres, proved by Charles Ward; Ordered registered.

Deed: Jesse Register to Shadrick Stallins for 123 acres, proved by William Wells; Ordered registered.

Joseph Grimes, Security & Bail for Snodon Pearse in suit of Joseph Register vs. Snodon Pearse, surrendered said Pearse to Court & was discharged; Ordered Sheriff to take Pearse into custody.

Granted Stephen Bradys petition to have his Mill as a Public Grist Mill & he be entitled to all priviledges & advantages as are allowed to persons keeping a Publick Mill.

William Wells, one of the Collectors of Taxes, rendered a further account of Supernumerys of Taxes by him collected: Archibald Pearse & Henry Jones - £1-18-6 which he has paid the Clerk, which with sums he returned at the last Term amounting to £15-15-8 is in the whole £17-14-2, £6-2-6 in tickets, after deducting his Commission for Collecting he has paid to Clerk £11-17-8 in money & £6-2-6 in tickets.

James Whaley, one of the Securities for Defendant in suit of Adm'r of Shuffield vs. David George, delivered Defendant to Court & was discharged; Defendant offers as Securities Frederick Barfield & Samuel Jones.

Ordered Ealse Lynough, Orphan of Francis Lynough, to Court to chuse a Guardian.

Grand Jury sworn: John Molten, foremen, Thomas Hill, Joseph Smith, William Hollingsworth, Nathan Fountain, Robert Sloan, David Sloan, Jacob Wells, James McIntire, William Stokes, Benjamin Tanner. Stephen Snell & John Clarke.

Ordered William Magee, Constable, to attend Grand Jury.

Bill of Sale: Edward Harris to James Spiller for a Negro Wench Lucy for £150, proved by John Hay, Esq.; Ordered registered.

Deed: James Gillespie & Watson Burton to Robert Dickson for 250 acres, Acknowledged; Ordered registered.

Ordered the Hands belonging to Grimes & Lockharts Mill shall clear the stream of Muddy Creek from the Mouth up to the Mill Tail so rafts may pass & that said Hands be exempt from working on the Roads.

Appointed Jesse Brown constable in room of William Burton.

John Molten & William Newton, Special Bail for John Newton in suit of William Edwards vs. John Newton, surrendered Defendant to Court & were discharged; Sheriff ordered to take said Newton into custody.

WEDNESDAY MORNING, Court met at 9 o'clock according to adjournment.

Present: Worshipfull William Houston, Robert Dickson, Samuel Houston, James Outlaw, Joseph Dickson, Kedar Bryan, James Gillespie, John Beck, Charles Ward, Esquires.

Appointed Joseph Dickson, Kedar Bryan & James Gillespie a Committee at last Term to settle account of Arthur Stokes, Adm'r of Philip Rouse, dec'd, Committee report that Arthur Stokes paid £68-9-1; Court concurred, Ordered report filed.

Deed: William Whitfield, Sr. to William Whitfield, Minor, 3 pieces of land, proved by William Whitfield, Jr.; Ordered registered.

Deed: William Whitfield, Sr. to Buckner Killegrew for 150 acres, proved by William Whitfield, Jr.; Ordered registered.

Deed: Auston Beesly & James Rogers to Solomon Beesly for 151 acres, proved by Thomas Carleton; Ordered registered.

Deed: Amos Parker to Auston Bryan for 100 acres, proved by Joseph Dickson; Ordered registered.

Ordered George Smith, Jr. be Overseer of Road in room of Lewis Bames [Barnes?].

Deed: George Smith to William Smith for 250 acres, proved by Michael Glisson; Ordered registered.

Granted petition of sundry Inhabitants to have a new road laid off & opened from Old Wilmington Road near Cooks Mill on south side of Stewarts Creek leading toward the Court House & join the Old Road that leads to Cross Roads where most convenient.

Ordered Joseph Dickson, Thomas James, Jacob Matthews, Thomas Carleton, John Carleton, James Rogers, Solomon Beesly, Alex'r Dickson, Arthur Mathews, Stephen Rogers, Edw'd Dickson, Abraham Molten, Kedar Bryan, John Armstrong, John Molten, they or any 12 be a Jury to lay off said road & report a plan to next Court.

Ordered William Magee, Constable, summon & convene said Jury at Stewarts Creek Bridge at any time the foreman of said Jury directs & that Robert Dickson Qualify said Jury.

Ordered Henry Faison, with his hands, shall work on Road under William Beck, Overseer.

Ordered Michael Kinnard be Overseer of Road in room of John Beck on North side of Goshen Swamp & have all hands as low as the Indico Branch.

Snodon Pearse being committed to the Sheriffs custody in discharge of his bail in suit of Joseph Register, offers as Security Joseph Grimes who is accepted.

Deed: George Smith to Michael Glisson for 100 acres, proved by William Smith; Ordered registered.

THURSDAY MORNING, Court met at 9 o'clock according to adjournment.

Present: Worshipfull Tho. Routledge, Robert Dickson, Joseph Dickson, Charles Ward, Kedar Bryan, James Outlaw, Daniel Teachy, Esquires.

Jury appointed last Court to lay off the New Road from lower Grove Bridge to Waine County line opposite William Reeves, have laid off said Road as follows: Beginning at Grove Bridge & running along the Old Road to foot of Charles Wards path near Archibald Carrs, from thence crossing Goshen Swamp near Charles Wards, thence crossing NorthEast near John Kornegays, thence to County line opposite William Reeves, which road said Jury have marked; Court concurred.

Ordered New Road divided into three seperate Districts: one on south side of Goshen Swamp & two on north side of Goshen Swamp as follows: Ordered George Cooper Overseer of said Road from middle of Main Run of Goshen Swamp to Main Road near Archibald Carrs & have following hands, William Kenans hands, George Cooper,Sr.s hands, Richard Cooper, David Cannon, Sr., John Best,Sr.s hands, John Fleming, David Quin, James Quin, Uriah Gurganus, Edward Sloan, Joseph Grimes hands, Charles Wards hands, Charles Brown, Christopher Martin, David Murdocks hands; Ordered Sampson Grimes be Overseer of said Road from middle of Main Run of Goshen Swamp to dividing ridge between Goshen & NorthEast & have the following hands, Tho. Bradly, Jesse Swinson, Joshua Chambles, Jesse Brock, John Rogers,Jr., John Winders, Cason Harris, Mich'l Sulliven, William Bullard, William Sulliven, Caleb Sulliven, Silas Carter, Richard Bradley, Samuel Bowden, William Taylor, John Rogers & sons, John Swinson, James Grimes, John Sulliven,Sr., Ruben Weston & sons, Step'n Herring, John Sulliven,Jr., John Mainer, James Taylor.

Ordered each of said Overseers proceed to open Road in Goshen Swamp & build a bridge over the Run, the first work they do.

Ordered Daniel Glisson be Collector of Taxes in District of Capt. Kenans & Capt. Bowdens Companies.

Appointed John Matchet Collector of Districts of Capt. Millers, Capt. Houstons & Capt. Outlaws Companies.

Appointed Auston Bryan Collector of Districts of Capt. Southerlands, Capt. Teachys, Capt. Stallins & Capt. Dicksons Companies.

Ordered each of said Collectors to give Bond of £1,000 with approved security & Clerk to file said Bonds.

Ordered James Winders be Overseer of Road in room of Thos. Hooks.

Appointed Daniel Teachy Guardian to Ealse Lynough, Orphan of Francis Lynough, dec'd; he gave Bond of £1,000; Ordered he take into his possession all Estate of said Orphan wherever he can find it.

Robert Dickson, Adm'r of Isom Shuffield, dec'd, rendered a receipt from John Huske to wit: Wilmington, May 9, 1786. Received from Robert Dickson, Esq. by hands of Mr. James Mills £31, the same being on account of Bond due by Estate of Isom Shuffield to Estate of Robert Hogg, for which sum credit is given on said Bond; Ordered said receipt filed.

William McGowen rendered account for funeral expenses of Mary White who died at his house & left no property to discharge her funeral expenses; Ordered said McGowen be paid by County Wardens £5 out of Parish Tax & account filed.

William McGowen rendered on Oath an inventory of all the effects of above said Mary White, amounting to £2-15-7; Ordered filed.

Ordered Edmond Dunkin, Sr. be Overseer of the New Road from Waine County line crossing NorthEast to the Ridge dividing the waters of the NorthEast from the waters of Goshen & have the following hands: Adam Reeves, Edm'd Dunkin, Jr., Isaac Dunkin, George Kornegay, Jr., John Kornegay, Rubin Johnston & son, William Hines, William Harris, William Dunkin, William O'Daniel, Ephram Shuffield, David Walker, Elisha Jones, Lewis Jones, Demsey Taylor, Daniel Parker, Jonathan Parker, John Whitehead, Demsey Westbrook, Bukford Garriss.

Ordered said Edmond Dunkin & hands meet at Goshen with the other Overseers & work with them till the Bridge is made & Causeway.

Samuel Houston returned list of Taxables for Capt. Hubbards Company.

Joseph T. Rhodes returned list of Taxables for Capt. Southerlands Company.

Daniel Teachy returned list of Taxables for Capt. Stallins Company.

Joseph Dickson returned list of Taxables for Capt. Gillespies Company.

Kedar Bryan returned list of Taxables for Capt. Kenans Company.

Charles Ward returned list of Taxables for Capt. Millers Company.

James Outlaw returned list of Taxables for Capt. Whiteheads Company.

William Taylor returned list of Taxables for Capt. Bowdens Company.

On hearing petition & answer in suit of Orphans of W. Stevens vs. William Stevens, Adm'r; Ordered Adm'r pay Guardian of said Orphans agreeable to settlement made by Commission of this Court in August, 1782, with interest to this date, £30 to Slocumb & 24 shillings to Mildred Stevens to be deducted.

John Cook & Andrew Wallace, bail for William Allen in suit of John Matchet vs. William Allen, surrendered said Allen & were discharged; Ordered Allen into Sheriffs custody.

FRIDAY MORNING, Court met at 9 o'clock according to adjournment.

Present: Worshipfull Tho. Routledge, Robert Dickson, Charles Ward, Sam'l Houston, James Gillespie, Thomas Hooks, Esquires.

It being suggested to this Court that Nathaniel Love, Inhabitant of this County, is in a state of Insanity; Ordered venieri shall issue to the Sheriff to convene a Jury of good & lawful men to inspect said Nathaniel Love & return their proceedings to next Court.

Allowed Thomas Hooks his account for services as Commissioner for setling the Court House, Goal, etc., amounting to £4.

Deed: Charles Miller to his daughter Mary Miller for a Negro wench & sundry articles, proved by Samuel Houston; Ordered registered.

It being suggested by some of the Commissioners for clearing the Run of Goshen that from continual rains during the present season which have kept the waters so high no work can be done to any effect & the high roads being much out of repair; Ordered the Commissioners, Overseers & hands directed to work on Run of Goshen or the Run of the NorthEast above William Kornegays Bridge be dischraged from working on them till the first of July next in order that the respective Overseers of the Roads may be enabled to repair the Roads.

Ordered Thomas Routledge, Samuel Houston, John Molten, Thomas James be Jurymen at next Superior Court at Wilmington the 6th day of December next.

Ordered John McCulloh, Jr., Wm. McGowen, James Dickson, Alex'r Dickson, Solomon Peesley, James Midleton (Grove), Robert Bishop, John Lanier, John Humphry, Charles Bostick, Wm. Nethercut, Sr., Stephen Martindel, Shadrick Sowell, Alexander Graddy, Andrew Gufford, Owen O'Daniel, William Kernegay, Shadrick Stallins, Aaron Williams, William Wells, William McCann, William McCann, Jr., Samuel Ward, Hillary Hooks, Thomas Wright, William Stevens, Willis Cherry, Tho. Flowers, Stephen Miller, David Murdock & John Neale, Sr. attend as Jurymen the next Court.

Ordered Benjamin Tanner be Overseer of Road in room of James McIntire.

Ordered Auston Bryan, Daniel Southerland & Abraham Newkirk be Searchers in District of Capt. Southerlands Company.

Ordered Solomon Beesly be Searcher in room of William McGowen, infirm & unable to serve.

Ordered Henry Allen, John Tilman, Joseph Bray, Sr., Benjamin Williams, John Ward, John Waller, John Knowles, Christopher Beck[?], being aged, poor & infirm, exempted from payment of Poll Tax for the future.

Ordered Road formerly laid off from Bull Tail to Main Road near Edward Dicksons be continued & William Beven be continued as Overseer & have same hands as formerly & that he proceed to open & repair said Road.

Allowed Samuel Ratliff 12 shillings for summoning & convening a Jury of Inquest on body of Anthony Baily, dec'd.

Allowed Charles Ward 24 shillings for holding Coroners Inquest on body of said Anthony Baily.

Allowed William Magee 12 shillings for summoning & convening a Jury of Inquest on body of Mary White, dec'd.

Allowed Charles Ward 24 shillings for holding Coroners Inquest on body of said Mary White.

The above allowances to be paid out of County Tax.

Upon motion of Mr. Gray, Ordered scitation issued Robert Dickson, Adm'r of Florance McCarty, dec'd, to shew cause why execution should not issue on a judgement obtained by Samuel Atkins against said Florence McCarty in his lifetime for £18 with costs.

Ordered Tax of one shilling laid & collected from every Poll Taxable person & one shilling on every 300 acres in this County for building a Bridge over the NorthEast River at or near the Mouth of Limestone Creek & that Collector of Public Taxes shall collect said Taxes & pay same to Commissioners appointed to superintend said Bridge.

Ordered James Gillespie, Robert Dickson, Joseph T. Rhodes be Commissioners to view & inspect the place & employ workmen to build said Bridge & superintend same.

Ordered Jesse George be Overseer in room of Andrew Thally.

Charles Ward & Samuel Houston, being a Committee to inspect the accounts of Joseph Dickson, County Trustee, report it appears that said Dickson hath paid away in several payments at several times £236-0-8 for which he has rendered vouchers; Ordered said account filed & vouchers destroyed, Court having concurred with said settlement.

Upon petition of sundry Inhabitants, Ordered a New Road laid off from NorthEast Bridge at William Kornegays to cross Goshen where most convenient & to lead to Grove Bridge near Col. Routledge & that Edward Pearsall, George Williams, Ivey Smith, George Smith, Joseph Smith, John Neale, John Matchet, Edward Houston, Lewis Barfield, Lewis Barnes, William Kornegay, John Houseman, Benja. Herring, Alexander Graddy, Frederick Graddy, William Hubbard, John Johnston, Archibald Carr & Joseph Wetts be a Jury to view & lay off said Road & report to next Court.

Ordered Loftis Worley, Constable, summon & convene said Jury & Charles Ward to Qualify said Jury.

Ordered James Winders be Overseer of Road in room of Thomas Hooks.

Ordered William Magee, Constable, be allowed 32 shillings for attending Court 4 days.

Allowed Daniel Glisson, Constable, 24 shillings for attending Court 3 days.

Court Adjourned Till Court in Course.

[signed] Tho. Routledge, Robert Dickson, Joseph Dickson, Cha. Ward, Sam'l Houston, James Gillespie.

15 January 1787 County Court Begun & Held for County of Duplin at the Court House, the 3rd Monday.

Present: Worshipfull William Houston, Thomas Routledge, Joseph T. Rhodes, Esquires.

Ordered John D[?], Orphan about 6 years of age last July, Bound Apprentice to Emanuel Bowzer till age 21 to learn the Trade of Black Smith & to read the Bible & write.

TUESDAY MORNING, Court met at 9 o'clock according to adjournment.

Present: Worshipfull William Houston, Tho. Routledge, Cha. Ward, Samuel Houston, Esquires.

Ordered Robert Twilly be constable in room of Loftis Worley.

Read petition of sundry persons on Rockfish praying to discontinue the New Road from Bull Tail to Edward Dicksons; Order for establishment of road reversed & road discontinued.

Dedimus from his Excellency Richard Caswell dated 6 Jan. 1787, directed to William Houston, Thomas Routledge & Robert Dickson & adding Francis Olliver, John Lanier, William Beck & Frederick Williams to the Commission of the Peace, whereupon said John Lanier & William Beck Qualified by taking Oaths & Oath of Justice of the Peace & took seats upon the Bench.

Grand Jury sworn: William McGowen, foreman, James Dickson, John McCulloh, Jr., Robert Bishop, Charles Bostick, Shadrick Sowell, Alexander Graddy, William Nethercut, Andrew Gufford, Owen O'Daniel, Aaron Williams, Sam'l Ward, Willis Cherry, Hillary Hooks, David Murdock, John Neale.

Ordered Loftis Worley, Constable, attend Grand Jury.

Joseph Williams, aged & infirm man having very little property, petitioned the Court to be exempted from being Taxed as a Poll for the future; Granted.

James Maxwell granted Adm'n on Estate of David Maxwell, dec'd, he offers as Securities William Carr & James Evens & gave Bond of £300 & took Oath of Admin'n.

WEDNESDAY MORNING, Court met at 9 o'clock according to adjournment.

Present: Worshipfull William Houston, Thomas Routledge, Joseph Dickson, Robert Dickson, Thomas Hooks, William Beck, Esquires.

Ordered Samuel Jones be Overseer of Road in room of Lewis Barnes & have same hands.

Ordered James Gillespie, William McGowen & Joseph Dickson be a Committee to settle & Adjust the accounts & claims of Heirs of John Cook, dec'd, & divide Estate among Heirs of said dec'd, agreeable to the Will & report to next Court.

Ordered Robert Dickson, Joseph Thomas Rhodes, Robert Southerland & Joseph Dickson, or any 3, be a Committee to settle accounts of Estate of Barnet Brock dec'd, between Abraham Newkirk & Heirs of said dec'd & report a true state thereof to the next Court.

As the Jury summoned to lay off a road between William Kornegays Bridge on the NorthEast & Grove Bridge has not proceeded thereon, Ordered same Jury be summoned & convened & that they proceed accordingly & Report to next Court.

Ordered Lavin Watkins be Overseer of Road in room of James Grimes.

Auston Bryan, charged with begeting a Bastard Child of Fereby Parker, gave Bond as required by Law for Indemnifying the Parish.

Lewis Jones, charged with begeting a Bastard Child of Ann Sulliven, gave Bond as required by Law.

Bill of Sale: George Haywood to John Woodward, Sr., for a Negro Peter for £100, proved by John Cook; Ordered registered.

Nicholas Hunter, Bail for Robert Williams in suit of Charles Brown vs. Robert Williams, Sr., surrendered said Williams & was discharged; Robert Williams, Jr. offered himself as Special Bail for Robert Williams, Sr. & is accepted.

William Hines, charged with begeting a Bastard Child of Prudance Taylor, gave Bond as required by Law for Indemnifying the Parish.

Ordered the following be noticed to attend the Next Court & bring with them the Orphan in their charge: Agga Sulliven & her two children, Archibald & Elkanah; Abe Taylor & his small child about 5 years old; Prudance Taylor & her small child; Joseph Hutson to bring Penelope White, an Orphan about 13 years old.

THURSDAY MORNING, Court met at 9 o'clock according to adjournment.

Present: Worshipfull Tho. Routledge, Robert Dickson, Charles Ward, Sam'l Houston, Thomas Hooks, James Outlaw, Esquires.

Robert Dickson, Adm'r of Isom Shuffield, dec'd, produced a receipt from John Huske, Attorney for Hogg & Campbell for £32-17-4 paid to said Huske for use of Hogg & Campbell on account of said Isom Shuffield, dec'd; Ordered filed.

Ordered summons issued Doctor Cocker & John Atkins to next Court to make objections, if any, to the building of a Public Grist Mill by Joseph Grimes over Cypress Creek, Grimes owning the land on one side of the Creek & Dr. Cocker or John Atkins the land on the other.

Ordered Joseph T. Rhodes, Samuel Houston, Auston Bryan, John Lanier, Robert Dickson, Richard Williams, James Picket, or any four, be a Committee to lay off & value one acre on each side of said stream for the purpose of building said Mill & report to next Court.

Ordered Clerk to purchase suitable Bound Books for keeping the accounts & records of Orphans Estates & that he draw upon the County Trustee for the money, which shall be alloed said Trustee in his settlement with the Court.

~~Written article of separation between Edward G. Debruhl & Mary Debruhl, his wife, Exhibited, proved by John Houseman; Ordered registered.~~

Deed: William Anderson to Philip Ward for sundry goods, proved by Benjamin Blount; Ordered registered.

Deed: Thomas Picket to John Parker for 50 acres, proved by James Picket; Ordered registered.

Deed: Richard Prescut to John Williams for 150 acres, proved by Loftis Worley; Ordered registered.

Deed: Joseph Bray /to John Williams for 200 acres, Acknowledged; Ordered registered.

Deed: Abraham Newton & Lois Newton to James Newton & Joshua Newton for 300 acres, proved by Daniel Aulderman; Ordered registered.

Deed: John Thomson to Moses Stanley for 300 acres, proved by Needham Whitfield; Ordered registered.

Deed: Nathan Newell to Moses Stanley for 300 acres, proved by Needham Whitfield; Ordered registered.

Deed: John Johnston to Hanch Johnston for 250 acres, Acknowledged; Ordered registered.

Deed: Robert Wilkinson to Luke Ward for 75 acres, proved by William Dickson; Ordered registered.

Deed: Henry Bulls to Patrick Newton for 150 acres, proved by Austin Moore; Ordered registered.

Deed: Dan Bowen to Elijah Bowen for 200 acres, proved by David Alderman; Ordered registered.

Deed: James Murray, Sr. to James Murray, Jr. for 100 acres, proved by William Picket; Ordered registered.

Deed: John Holden to James Carr for 240 acres, proved by Robert Sloan; Ordered registered.

Deed: Robert Merrit to David Davis for 200 acres, proved by James Rollings; Ordered registered.

Deed: John Winders to James Winders for 2 pieces of land, proved by James Ward; Ordered registered.

Deed: John Winders to Jesse Swinson for 100 acres, proved by James Ward; Ordered registered.

Deed: Joseph Dickson to John Blanton for 100 acres, Acknowledged; Ordered registered.

Deed: Alexander Dickson to James Carr for 100 acres, Acknowledged; Ordered registered.

Deed: John Tucker to John Evans for 150 acres, proved by John Mathews; Ordered registered.

Ordered the following summoned to next Court to give account of their Guardianship of Orphans committed to their charges:
Joseph Dickson, Guardian of Wm. Williams;
Auston Bryan, Guardian of James Picket;
Robert Dickson, Guardian of Shuffields Orphans;
Charles Ward, Guardian of Matchets Orphans;
Abra'm Newkirk, Guardian of Brocks Orphans;
Thomas Hooks, Guardian of Slocumbs Orphans;
William Kenan, Guardian of Blackmoores Orphans;
Patrick Newton, Guardian of Moores Orphans;
John Houseman, Guardian of Moores Orphans;
Warrin Blount, Guardian of McCallops Orphans;
John Cook, Guardian of Cooks Orphans;
William Hubbard, Guardian of Worleys Orphans
Dan'l Teachy, Guardian of Lynoughs Orphan;
Mildred Stevens, Guardian of Stevens Orphans.

FRIDAY MORNING, Court met at 9 o'clock according to adjournment.

Present: Worshipfull William Houston, Thomas Routledge, Charles Ward, Joseph Dickson, James Gillespie, Esquires.

Joseph Johnston, Garnishee to Henry E. McCulloh, settled principal & interest due upon his Bond & paid Sheriff £23-9-0 & there appears a Ballance now due upon his said Bond after such payment of £31-6-3.

Deed: John Molten to Joseph Cox, Jr. for 250 acres, proved by James Dickson; Ordered registered.

Article of Agreement between James Lockhart in behalf of his children & Joseph Grimes Exhibited, proved by James Gillespie; Ordered registered.

As last Court Ordered laying off a New Road to lead from the Old Wilmington Road near Cooks Mill on the south side of Stewarts Creek leading towards the Court House & joining the Old Road leading to the Cross Roads where most convenient, which Order has never been put into execution; Ordered that Joseph Dickson, Thomas James, Jacob Matthews, Thomas Carleton, James Rogers, Alexander Dickson, Solomon Beesly, Arthur Matthews, Stephen Rogers, Edward Dickson, Abraham Molten, John Molten, Kedar Bryan, John Armstrong, James Midleton, Sr., James Gillespie & Auston Beesly, or any 12, be a Jury to lay off said Road & report to next Court.

Ordered William Magee, Constable, summon & convene said Jury at Stewarts Creek Bridge when directed by Robert Dickson who is to Qualify said Jury.

Ordered Isaac Newton, Orphan 15 years of age, Bound Apprentice to John Goff,Jr. to learn trade of Wheel Wright.

Ordered Joseph Grimes, Adm'r of Pearses Estate, to appear at next Court & render account of said Admin'n.

Ordered William Southerland & Daniel Southerland, Guardians of the Orphans of Francis Buie, to appear at next Court & render account of their Guardianship.

The Jury to inspect & inquire into the condition of Nathaniel Love, returned the verdict that they consider Love to be in a state of Insanity or Lunacy; Court appointed Gen'l James Kenan Guardian to said Love, he gave Bond of £300 & approved security; Ordered said James Kenan to take into his possession the Estate of said Love where ever he can find it.

In pursuance to an Act of the General Assembly passed at Newbern in December, 1785, to establish an Academy in Duplin by name of Grove Academy, Thomas Routledge, James Kenan, William Dickson, Joseph Dickson, James Gillespie, five of the Trustees of the Academy appointed by the Assembly, gave Bond as required by Law; Ordered Bond registered.

Ordered following summoned to next Court as Jurymen: Theophilus Williams, Lavin Watkins, George Kornegay, Michael Kinard, Benjamin Johnston, Wm. Sulliven, Thomas Hill, Patrick Newton, James Morris, John Chambers, Arch'd Carr, Robert Williams, Loftis Worley, John Southerland,Jr., Caleb Quin, Jesse Lanier, James Picket, Henry Picket, John Waller, William Hall, James Maxwell, James Murray, William Frederick, Stephen Rogers, Thomas Heath, Joseph Williams,Jr., John Goff,Jr., Mesheck Stallins, Thomas James, John Boney, Richard Chasen, John Avers, William Kornegay, Benjamin Herring, John Glisson & Ruben Weston.

In suit of Arthur Stokes, Admin'r vs. Wm. Allen & others, former judgement of the Court was for £29-7-11; It is now the opinion of the Court that Allens securities were good & sufficient at the time the debt was contracted, therefore the Admin'r is not liable for above judgement & Guardian shall receive same.

Ordered Edward Pearsall Overseer of Road in room of John Matchet.

Ordered Anthony Miller Overseer of Road in room of William Hubbard.

James Dickson rendered his account for three Books he purchased for Registering Deeds amounting to £3-17-0; Court allowed this & Ordered County Trustee to pay him same & take his receipt which shall be good in his settlement with the Court.

William Dickson, Clerk of this Court, produced Treasurers receipt for copies of 17 Sheriff's Bonds which he transmitted to the Treasurers Office in pursuance to Treasurers letter demanding same; Ordered said Dickson allowed £7-4-0, being fees allowed for that service, to be paid out of County Tax.

Allowed William Dickson, Clerk of this Court, £15 for extra services the last year.

Allowed James Kenan, Sheriff of this County, £15 out of County Tax for extra services for last year, being first year of his Sheriffalty.

Appointed James Gillespie Guardian to Lincoln Shuffield, Orphan of Ison Shuffield, dec'd, Gillespie gave Bond of £300; Ordered he take said Estate into his hands where he can find it.

Robert Dickson Exhibited petition in behalf of himself & wife praying that James Gillespie, Guardian of Lincoln Shuffield, be seited to appear at next Court to shew cause, if any, why Dower should not be Granted agreeable to prayers of said petition; Granted.

Ordered John Lanier, James Picket, Wm. Hollingsworth, Robert Cole, John Farrier, Wm. Farrier, Robert Cottle, Nathan Fountain, Lamuel Lanier, Solomon Picket, Henry Fountain, Amos Parker, John Williams, Joel Wilder & Moses Thoaler be a Jury to lay off a road leading from Muddy Creek Road to cross Black Swamp Road to meet the Onslow Road at the most convenient place & report to next Court.

Ordered Jesse Brown, Constable, to summon & convene & Joseph T. Rhodes to Qualify said Jury.

Court Adjourned Till Court in Course.

[signed] Wm. Houston, Sr., Tho. Routledge, Robert Dickson, Cha. Ward, Joseph Dickson, James Gillespie.

JANUARY COURT, 1787

The following is a list of the several species of Taxes to be collected by the Several Collecters in Duplin County for the year 1786, by the Collecters now appointed:

General Tax	each Poll or 300 acres	15/ -
Co. Conting's	"	1/ -
Court House	"	1/ -
No. E't Bridge	"	1/ -
Poor Tax	"	1/ -
Dist. Goal Tax	"	1/ - 6
Sinking Fund	"	1/ - 6

General Tax may ½ be paid in certificates.

15 March, 1787

Special Court Begun & Held at the Court House, Thursday.

For the immediate tryal of Darby & Peter, two Negro Slaves, property of the late William Taylor, Esquire, now committed & to be tryed for the murder of said William Taylor, their Master. Court being summoned & convened by the Sheriff, Qualified.

Present: Thomas Routledge, Joseph Dickson, James Gillespie, Esquires & Justices; Lewis Thomas, James Midleton, Sr., Isaac Hunter, Alexander Dickson, Freeholders; all being owners of Slaves & unexceptional according to Law.

The said Negro, Darby, did confess that he did on the 13th day of Inst. March felloniously & maliciously & wilfully murder William Taylor by striking him on the head with an ax into his Brain, of which wound his said Master instantly died; Court Ordered Darby immediately committed to Goal under a good guard & on tomorrow between one & four o'clock in the afternoon he be taken out & tied to a stake on the Court House lott & there burned to death & to ashes & his ashes strewd upon the ground.

Said Peter, age about 14, did confess that he was present when his Master, the said William Taylor, was murdered & that he did aid & assist his brother, Darby, in commiting said Murder; Court having taken into consideration the youth of said Peter & considering him under the influence of his older brother, Darby, passed the following sentence: said Peter be committed to Goal & remain under good guard till tomorrow & then between one & four o'clock be taken out & tied to a Post on the Court House Lott & there to have ½ of each of his ears cut off & be branded on each cheek with the letter M & receive 100 lashes on his bare back.

To which sentences the Court have hereto subscribed their names. [signed] Tho. Routledge, Joseph Dickson, James Gillespie, Lewis Thomas, James Middleton, Isaac Hunter, Alexander Dickson. Test. W.Dickson, C.C.

16 April, 1787, County Court Begun & Held for County of Duplin at the Court House, the 3rd Monday.

Present: Worshipfull William Houston, Thomas Routledge, James Gillespie, Esquires.

Exempted Nathaniel Edwards, aged & having no property, from payment of Taxes as a Poll.

John Cocke produced licence from the Judge of the Superior Courts of Law & Equity authorizing him to Plead & Practise as an Attorney, took Oath of Qualification & his seat at the Barr.

Ordered John Chambers excused from serving as Juryman this Term.

TUESDAY MORNING, Court met at 9 o'clock according to adjournment.

Present: Worshipfull Tho. Routledge, Robert Dickson, Charles Ward, Samuel Houston, Kedar Bryan, Esquires.

Ordered George Kornegay be Overseer of Road in room of Jacob Kornegay.

Exempted John Murrow, poor & aged & having no property, from payment of Taxes as a Poll.

Grand Jury sworn: Theophilus Williams, foreman, William Frederick, Thomas Heath, Benjamin Herring, Richard Chasen, Thomas Hill, Patrick Newton, Archibald Carr, John Southerland, Jesse Lanier, James Murray, Joseph Williams, John Boney, Reuben Weston.

Ordered William Magee, Constable, attend Grand Jury.

Ordered Rich'd Bradley, Thomas Bradley, Jesse Swinson, Solomon Rogers, Micajah Rogers, Jesse Branch, Burwell Branch, William Salmon added to District of Roads where Lavin Watkins is Overseer & work under him.

Exempted Joseph Twilly, aged & having no property, also William Savage & James Willson, aged & poor, from payment of Taxes as a Poll.

Mesheck Stallins excused from serving as Juryman this Court.

Ordered Jonas Bailey, Orphan age 14 the first of January last past, Bound Apprentice to Solomon Beesly till age 21 to learn trade of a Shoe Maker & to read & write.

Exhibited settlement of Estate of Barnet Brock, dec'd, between Abraham Newkirk, Admin'r, & Orphans of the dec'd; Ordered filed.

Granted Catherine Taylor, widow of William Taylor, dec'd, & John Rhodes Admin'n on Estate of said Taylor; they gave Security of £1,000 & took Oath.

Catherine Taylor Exhibited following deposition: State of North Carolina, Duplin County, April 17, 1787 - Samuel Bowden & Richard Bradley, being duly sworn, sayeth that some few days after the marriage of James McCulloh with Mary Taylor, daughter to the late William Taylor, dec'd, they saw the said William Taylor deliver to the said James McCulloh a Negro Slave Dinah, upon which the said McCulloh took the said Negro Woman from Mr. Taylors hand & delivered her to Mrs. Catherine Taylor, wife of the said William Taylor, dec'd, to be her property during her natural life & further these Deponants sayeth not. Samuel Bowden (Seal), Richard Bradley (Seal). Sworn to before me the date above, Joseph Dickson,J.P.

Ordered Samuel Sowell be Overseer of Road in room of Thos. Quinn.

Ordered Owen O'Daniel be Overseer in room of Frederick Grady.

Deed: William Picket,Sr. to William Picket,Jr. for two pieces of land, proved by James Murray,Sr.; Ordered registered.

Francis Olliver,Esq., one of the Justices named in the Commission of the Peace bearing date 6 January 1787, took Oath of Qualification of Officers & of a Justice of the Peace & took his seat upon the Bench.

James Conner, Orphan Mullatto, was Bound at the April Term, 1786 to Abraham Molten,Jr., it now appears said Conner was previously Bound by County Court of Dobbs County to Henry Goodman of Dobbs County; Court now declares Indentures binding said child to said Molten nul & void.

Exempted Douglas Powell, aged, poor man, from payment of Taxes as a Poll.

WEDNESDAY MORNING, Court met at 9 o'clock according to adjournment.

Present: Worshipfull William Houston, Charles Ward, Joseph Dickson, John Lanier, Sam'l Houston, Esquires.

Granted James Pearsall licence to keep an Ordinary in his own house, he offered as Securities Joseph Dickson & Robert Twilly.

Granted William Frederick licence to keep an Ordinary at his own house, he offered as Securities Daniel Glisson & Ivey Smith.

Granted William Best licence to keep an Ordinary at his own house, he offered as Securities Robert Twilly & Daniel Glisson.

Exhibited additional Inventory of Estate of Jesse Barfield, dec'd; Ordered filed.

Ordered William Dickson, Thomas Hooks & Dan'l Glisson be a Committee to settle accounts of Estate of Jesse Barfield, dec'd, between Admin'r & Heirs of said dec'd & report to next Court.

Elisabeth Lawhan, Single woman, made Oath that she has at her own expense cloathed & maintained her Bastard Child begotten by Absalom Mercer for 15 months for which she has never received any satisfaction; Court adjudged said Mercer shall pay her 10 shillings per month for aforesaid term & Ordered Clerk furnish her with a copy of the Order.

Exhibited the Last Will & Testament of John Graddy, proved by Bryan Whitfield, one of the subscribing evidences; Fred'k Graddy, named as Executor in said Will, Qualified.

Granted Isaac Hunter licence to keep an Ordinary at his own house, he offered as Securities William Hubbard & William Hall.

Jury appointed last Court to lay off a New Road from William Kornegays Bridge on the NorthEast crossing Goshen to the Grove Bridge, reported the Road laid off & marked.

Ordered that as Jesse Brown by mistake gave an Infant to be a Poll Tax, he be discharged from payment & Collecter be allowed same in his list of Insolvents.

Ordered William Curtis, Orphan age about 13, Bound Apprentice to Joseph Williams for 7 years, to learn trade of Shoe Maker & to read & write.

The Committee appointed last Court to view & value one acre of land on each side of Cypress Creek where Joseph Grimes was granted liberty to build a Publick Grist Mill where said Grimes owns land on the north side of the Creek & Dr.Cocker or John Atkins owns land on the south side, have met & laid off one acre on the south side of said Creek, beginning at a pine on the hill & runs S65 W75 yards to a stake, thence S25 E75 yards to a stake, thence N65 E70 yards to beginning, valued at 25 shillings; said Committee also valued to 15 shillings one acre on the north side of the Creek opposite the other; total evaluation of the two acres amounting to £2 which money is in the hands of the Clerk; Report signed by said Committee, John Lanier, James Picket, Richard Williams; Ordered filed.

Ordered Arthur Stokes discharged from payment of Taxes on 200 acres which he appears to be overcharged with in his list for 1786 & that Collecter be allowed same in settlement of his Insolvents.

Exhibited Last Will & Testament of Timothy Murphy, proved by Jacob Wells & William Wells, two of subscribing witnesses; Ordered filed.

Ordered Frederick Barfield, Admin'r of Jesse Barfield, dec'd, to sell remainder of Perishable part of Estate in order to discharge debts & report to next Court.

James Roberts, being charged by Sarah Alberson with begeting her Bastard Child & being bound over to Court, came before the Court & entered into recognizance in the sum of £100 & John Houseman & Ivey Smith, his Securities, in the sum of £50 each for Indemnifying the Parish from maintenance of said Child.

THURSDAY MORNING, Court met at 9 o'clock according to adjournment.

Present: Worshipfull Wm. Houston, Tho. Routledge, Robert Dickson, Charles Ward, Joseph Dickson, Kedar Bryan, William Beck, Thomas Hooks, Sam'l Houston, Esquires.

Mildred Stevens, Admin'x, Exhibited an account current with the Estate of William Stevens, dec'd, balance of £382 in her hands belonging to Alice, Suckey & Charles Stevens, Orphans of said dec'd; Ordered filed.

As the Order to the Sheriff at the last Court to convene a Jury to lay off 1/3 of the lands which did belong to Francis Brice in his lifetime to Abigal Brice, widow of said Francis Brice, dec'd, has not been carried into effect; Court again Ordered Sheriff to convene a Jury of twelve men upon the premises now in dispute between Simon Davis & Abigal Brice to lay off 1/3 of lands formerly belonging to said Francis Brice & at the same time the Sheriff put said Abigal Brice into possession of said 1/3 part of lands as her Dower.

Inventory of William Campbell, dec'd, Exhibited by Michael Sulliven, Admin'r; Ordered filed.

Ordered Samuel Houston to certifie & return warrant & Proceedings of Tryal held before him between Simon Davis & Abigal Brice to this Term, the matter being settled before the Court; Ordered Clerk issue a Supersedeas to Robert Twilly, the Constable, directing he proceed no farther in executing said judgement & deliver goods executed to Mrs. Brice.

Deed: Isaac Dawson to Alex'r Graddy for 150 acres, proved by Frederick Graddy; Ordered registered.

Deed: George Cooper to John Cooper for 250 acres, proved by Benjamin Best; Ordered registered.

Deed: Jeremiah Hulet to Solomon Carter for 100 acres, proved by Solomon Picket; Ordered registered.

Deed: William Wilkins to Edward Cornwallis Dibruhl for 200 acres, proved by Frederick Barfield; Ordered registered.

Deed: Christopher Martin to Henry Stokes for 180 acres, Acknowledged; Ordered registered.

Deed: William Graddy to Alexander Graddy for 100 acres, proved by Frederick Graddy; Ordered registered.

Deed: John Neale to Andrew Reed for 100 acres, proved by Robert Lester; Ordered registered.

Deed: John Rivenbark to John Boney for 100 acres, proved by Daniel Teachy; Ordered registered.

Deed: George Outlaw to Lavin Watkins for 125 acres, proved by Francis Olliver; Ordered registered.

Deed: James Hurst, Jr. to Lavin Watkins for 60 acres, proved by Francis Olliver; Ordered registered.

Deed: James Hurst to Lavin Watkins for 5 acres, proved by Francis Olliver; Ordered registered.

Deed: Rice Matthews to Mesheck Stallins for 200 acres, proved by William Wells; Ordered registered.

Deed: Hicks Mills to Benjamin Dulany for 100 acres, proved by John Morrow; Ordered registered.

Deed: Absalom Boyet to John Williams for 75 acres, Acknowledged; Ordered registered.

Deed: Thomas Clarke to Shadrick Stallins for 320 acres, proved by John Holden; Ordered registered.

Deed: Thomas Clarke to Shadrick Stallins for 50 acres, proved by John Holden; Ordered registered.

Deed: Ruban Weston to Samuel Bowden for 320 acres, Acknowledged; Ordered registered.

Deed: William Taylor to his daughter Elisabeth Taylor for sundry lands, proved by John Gibbs; Ordered registered.

Deed: William Taylor to his daughter Elisabeth Taylor for sundry Negroes & sundry stock, etc., proved by John Gibbs; Ordered registered.

Ordered William Dickson be Guardian to Catharin Cade, Orphan of Stephen Cade, dec'd, & take possession of her Estate where he can find it; he gave Bond of £300.

Michael J. Kenan, Entry Officer of Claims for Lands in Duplin County, returned to Court the following disputed Claim: #247 John Duff enters 100 acres in Duplin on East side of Rockfish joining Thomas Green, William James, Simon Rivenbark & Benjamin Fussells lines 17 Jan. 1787; John Green enters claim for 100 acres in Duplin County on East side of Rockfish joining Thomas Green, William James, Simon Rivenbark & Benjamin Fussells lines 19 Feb. 1787; True copy from Entry Book, M.J. Kenan; Ordered Sheriff convene a Jury upon Premises to try the above disputed claim & return proceedings to next Court.

Exempted Thomas Winders who has lost the use of his limbs & is unable to get his living by labor, from payment of Taxes as a Poll in the future till he recovers his health.

Mr. Thomas Hooks, Guardian to Orphans of John Charles Slocumb, dec'd, prayed an Order to sell a Negro Wench Jin belonging to the Estate of said Slocumb, dec'd, to enable him to make a proper settlement; Ordered he sell said Negro Wench at six months credit to highest bidder & report said sale to next Court.

Michael Sulliven, Admin'r of William Campbell, dec'd, Granted an Order to sell a Commissioners Certificate of £80-13-3 which is due from the Publick to said Campbell, at Publick Vendue for ready money to enable him to discharge such debts as may have been incurred in consequence of his said Admin'n of said Campbell & make report to next Court.

Upon motion of Mr.Gray, Court reconsidered judgement obtained in this Court by William Rigley against Edward Dickson & set aside said judgement & the execution issued thereon to be void; Ordered Clerk to transpose said suit on the Appearance Docket to next Court under same Rule of Reference as before.

Deed: William Kenan to Felix Frederick for 100 acres, proved by Christopher Martin; Ordered registered.

FRIDAY MORNING, Court met at 9 o'clock according to adjournment.

Present: Worshipfull William Houston, Tho. Routledge, Robert Dickson, Joseph Dickson, Charles Ward, Sam'l Houston, James Gillespie, Kedar Bryan, Esquires.

Whereas an Order made last Court to lay off a new road from Muddy Creek Road to cross back Swamp & meet the Onslow Road at the most convenient place has not been put into execution; Ordered Job Thigpen, Richard Williams, James Murray, William Picket, John Lanier, Henry Picket, Amos Parker, Robert Cole, Nathan Fountain, Henry Fountain, Solomon Picket, William Hollingsworth, James Picket, Abraham Andrews, John Williams, Jesse Lanier be a Jury to lay off said road & report a plan to next Court.

Ordered Jesse Brown, Constable, summon & convene & Joseph Thomas Rhodes Qualify said Jury.

Ordered James Gillespie, Joseph Thomas Rhodes, John Molten & Isaac Hunter be Jurymen to next Superior Court at Wilmington the 6th June next.

Ordered Nathaniel McCann be Overseer of NorthEast River from mouth at Rockfish up to Indian Grave Bluff & have same hands as formerly.

Ordered William Hollingsworth be Overseer of NorthEast River from Indian Graves up to Brocks Landing & that Nathan Fountain Andrew Wallace, James Cox, William Tegue, James Picket,Jr., Henry Fountain,

Jonathan Baker, William Picket,Jr. & Negro Quash, James Murray,Jr. work under him.

Ordered Abraham Newkirk be Overseer of NorthEast River from Brooks Landing up to Rogers Landing & that Ebenezer Garrison, Nicholas Sandlin, William New, Henry Newkirk, Thomas Canaday, Robert Bishop, Derry McIntire, Gillespies Sam, McGowens Peter, Dicksons Sip work under him.

Ordered Edward Houston be Overseer of NorthEast River from Rogers Landing up to George Millers Lagoon & that John Neale, Jr., Jacob Williams, William Hawthorn, Francis Whaley, Anthony Millers Will, Wm. Nethercut,Jr., Charles Sowell, John Southerland, Doct.Houstons Ned, Sam'l Houstons Charles, Fred'k Smith & Abraham Wilkings work under him.

Ordered William Kornegay be Overseer of NorthEast River from George Millers Lagoon up to William Kornegays Bridge & that Frederick Graddy, James Williams,Jr., Thomas Shelton, Frederick Smith, Jacob Mainer, Hubbards Boson, John Williams Arthur & Jack, James Herrings Ned & Bob work under him.

Ordered Joseph Thomas Rhodes, Samuel Houston & Robert Dickson be a Committee to inspect, direct & superintend clearing of said NorthEast from mouth of Rockfish up to William Kornegays Bridge & report from time to time to Court.

Ordered Samuel Sowell be Overseer of NorthEast Run or River from William Kornegays Bridge up to Solomon Carters footway & have his own Company of hands that worked under him on the Road & that he proceed to work on said Run or River with said Company.

Ordered Lewis Hines be Overseer of NorthEast Run or River from Solomon Carters footway up to James Outlaws Bridge & have same hands as formerly, his own Company & James Mathews Company except John Mainer & Besent Brock & that he proceed to work on said Run or River with said Companies.

Ordered William Hubbard, James Outlaw & Frederick Barfield be a Committee to superintend, direct & inspect said Business, etc. & report from time to time to Court.

Ordered Stephen Miller be Overseer of Lower District of Goshen from Mouth up to uper end of District that was formerly John Matchets & that he have all the hands that did formerly work under him & John Matchet.

Ordered Owen O'Daniel continued as Overseer of Second District in Goshen where Stephen Herring was formerly Overseer & have same hands belonging to said District.

Ordered Uriah Gurganus continued as Overseer of Third District in Goshen where Joseph Grimes was formerly Overseer & have same hands belonging to said Company.

Ordered David Cannon continued as Overseer of Fourth District of Goshen as formerly & have same hands belonging to said District.

Ordered Sampson Grimes continued as Overseer of Fifth District of Goshen as formerly & have same hands belonging to said District.

Ordered George Miller, Joseph Grimes & John Matchet be a Committee to direct, superintend & inspect said work & report from time to time to Court.

Ordered William Sulliven be Overseer of Sixth District of Goshen from lower end of Wards Slew to uper end of Grimes Slew & have same Company of hands as formerly belonged to said District.

Ordered John Sulliven continued as Overseer of Seventh District in Goshen which is above Grimes Slew & have same hands as formerly belonged to said District.

Ordered Thomas Hooks, Jr. be Overseer of Eighth District in Goshen & have same hands which formerly belonged to said District when under William Hooks as Overseer.

Ordered James Wright be Overseer of Ninth District in Goshen & have same hands belonging to said District as formerly.

Ordered Lavin Watkins continued as Overseer of Tenth District in Goshen & have same hands as formerly belonged to said District.

Ordered Cullen Connerly be Overseer of Eleventh District in Goshen & have same hands that Formerly belonged to said District under Theo. Williams.

Ordered Thomas Hooks, Lewis Thomas & Nicholas Bowden be a Committee to direct, superintend & inspect said work & report from time to time to the Court.

Ordered Daniel Glisson continued as Overseer of Twelfth District in Goshen & have same hands as formerly belonged to said District.

Ordered Willis Cherry continued as Overseer of Thirteenth District in Goshen & have the same hands as formerly belonged to said District which District is now to extend only from uper end of Cannons Slew to uper end of Sam Wards Slew.

Ordered John Bradley continued as Overseer of Fourteenth District in Goshen, that is from uper end of Sam Wards Slew to the Bridge on the South side of Goshen & that he have the same hands which formerly belonged to his District.

Ordered Hillary Hooks continued as Overseer of Fifthteenth District of Goshen, which is from the Main Run a little below the Middle Bridge up to a fork of the Run opposite a point of land that extends into the Swamp from the uper end of William Dicksons Peach Orchard & have the same hands as formerly belonged to said District.

Ordered William Beck continued as Overseer of the Sixteenth or uper District in Goshen from uper Landing down to Hillary Hooks District & have same hands of his former District.

Ordered John Beck, Wm. Dickson & Theophilus Williams be a Committee to direct, superintend & inspect the work of said uper five Districts & report from time to time to Court.

Ordered Overseers & hands now appointed to work on the NorthEast River & Goshen shall not be discharged from working on the Road till 20th July next nor be compelled to work on the NorthEast River or Goshen till after that time for which purpose the said Overseers are to receive their directions from the several Committees appointed for that purpose.

As James Dickson hath this Term obtained a judgement against Thomas Routledge for £57-7-2½ from which judgement the Defend't prayed an appeal which was granted, the Defendant withdrew his said appeal & consented the Judgement should stand as Recorded & by consent of Parties execution is stayed till after 25th October next.

Ordered Robert Twilly, Constable, allowed 24 shillings out of County Tax for attending Court 3 days.

Ordered William Magee, Constable, allowed 24 shillings for attending Court 3 days.

Ordered Daniel Glisson, Constable, allowed 40 shillings for attending Court 5 days last Court.

Ordered William Magee, Constable, allowed 40 shillings for attending Court 5 days last Court.

Ordered Lewis Thomas & John Hills hands work on the New Road under George Cooper, Overseer.

Ordered James Wright, Thomas Wright, Daniel Hicks, Dan'l Clarke, Alex'r Wilson, John Winders, Sr., John Bradley, Jesse Swinson, Sam'l Bowden, Thomas Bennet, John Williams (BC), Wm. Hubbard, Lewis Barfield, Stephen Miller, Edward Pearsall, R't Williams, Fred'k Graddy, Owen O'Daniel, Sampson Grimes, Wm. Whitfield, Edward Dickson, John Armstrong, Nicholas Hunter, William Rigby, Eph'm Garrison, William Carr, Lewis Brock, James McIntire, John Waller, Daniel Southerland, Richard Williams, Wm. Farrior, Meshack Stallins, William Wells, John Goff, David Sloan, Nath'l McCann, Wimbert Boney be Jurymen to next July Term.

Ordered William Sulliven, Sam'l Ward & James Morris be Searchers for Districts of Capt. Kenans Company.

Ordered Theophilus Williams, Nicholas Bowden & Elisha Jernigan be Searchers for District of Capt. Bowdens Company.

Ordered William Hubbard, Loftis Worley & Edward Houston be Searchers for District of Capt. Houstons Company.

Ordered Thomas Routledge have priviledge to build House or Bar for entertaining persons on Publick times on the Court House Lott.

James Kenan, William Dickson & Joseph Dickson, Ex'rs of the Last Will & Testament of Timothy Murphy, Qualified by taking Oath.

Court Adjourned Till Court in Course.

[signed] Wm. Houston, Sr., Tho. Routledge, Cha. Ward, James Gillespie, Joseph Dickson, Sam'l Houston.

16 July, 1787, County Court Begun & Held for County of Duplin at the Court House, the 3rd Monday.

Present: Worshipfull Tho. Routledge, Sam'l Houston, John Lanier, Esquires.

Granted Admin'n to Thomas Gray on Estate of Benjamin Dawson, dec'd; Gray gave Bond of £100.

Appointed Tho. Routledge, John Lanier & Fred'k Williams a Committee to settle accounts of Estate of Demsey Canaday, dec'd, with Executors of said dec'd & report to Court during this Term.

Frederick Williams, Esquire, appointed by last General Assembly a Justice of the Peace for Duplin County & named in the Commission of the Peace & Dedimus under hand & Seal of the Governor, Qualified by taking Oath for Qualification of Public Officers & Oath of a Justice of the Peace.

Samuel Jones, Jr. overcharged with 532 acres in 1786 which is more than he did possess or give in for that year; Ordered the Collecter deduct the Taxes on 532 acres to said Jones, which sum Collecter be allowed in settling his accounts for Insolvents.

Appointed John Matthews constable for District of Capt. Stallins Company; he gave Bond with approved Security & took Oath of Constable.

TUESDAY MORNING, Court met at 9 o'clock according to adjournment.

Present: Worshipfull Tho. Routledge, Charles Ward, John Lanier, Fred'k Williams, Esquires.

William Henry Hill, Esquire, produced a licence from two of the Judges of the Super'r Court of Law to practice as an Attorney in the Different County Courts of this State; he took Oath of an Attorney & was admitted accordingly.

Inventory of Estate of Ben Dawson, dec'd, Exhibited by Tho. Gray, Admin'r; Ordered filed.

Ordered Tho's Gray, Admin'r of Benjamin Dawson, dec'd, have leave to sell Estate of said dec'd & report to next Term.

Inventory of Estate of John Graddy, dec'd, Exhibited by Fred'k Grady, Ex'r; Ordered filed.

William Frederick prayed to have his Mill on the Plantation where he lives, recorded as a Public Grist Mill & allowed all bebefits the Law allows to persons who keep Public Grist Mills; Granted.

Grand Jury sworn: Edward Pearsall, foreman, William Rigby, William Whitfield, Thomas Wright, David Sloan, Nathaniel McCann, John Williams, Nicholas Hunter, John Armstrong, Sampson Grimes, John Goff, Jesse Swinson, Thomas Bennet, Fred'k Graddy & Samuel Bowden.

Ordered William Magee, Constable, attend Grand Jury.

Inventory of Estate of David Maxwell, dec'd, Exhibited by James Maxwell, Admin'r; Ordered filed.

Inventory of Estate of William Taylor, dec'd, Exhibited; Ordered filed.

Bill of Sale: David Bunting to George Cooper, Sr. for a Negro Woman Slave, Ruth, proved by Richard Cooper; Ordered registered

John Molten made Oath he was duly returned a Juror from this Court to last Wilmington Superior Court in June, 1787 & he attended said Court & obtained a Certificate from the Clerk of said Court for ten days attendance which was
at 8/ p. day   £4-0-0
 ?   1-8
Traveling, going &
   returning   1-12-0
          £5-13-8
For the Ticket   -8
          £5-14-4
Which said Certificate said John Molten declared he lost; Ordered Clerk furnish said Molten with a copy of this amount attested & that County Trustee pay him said amount & receive Clerks Certificate for a Voucher for same.

Bill of Sale: William Cole to Daniel Southerland, dated 4 May, 1787 for one mare & yearling, proved by Abraham Newkirk; Ordered registered.

Ordered Phil Southerland & James Midleton, Jr. added to Abraham Newkirk, Overseer of River.

Ordered Robert Dickson, Thomas Hooks, Francis Olliver, Jos. T. Rhodes & W. Dickson, or any three, be a Committee to divide the Estate of William Taylor, dec'd, between the Widow & Heirs of said dec'd & report to next Court.

Ordered Elisha Williford & James Pickets Peter added to William Hollingsworth, Overseer of the River.

Appointed Fred'k Barfield Guardian to John Barfield, Orphan, he gave Bond of £200.

Bill of Sale: Lavin King to William Dickson, dated 28 Nov. 1786 for two Negroes, Stephen & Liddia, proved by James Morris; Ordered recorded & registered.

Bill of Sale: Theophilus Williams to John Barfield for a Negro girl, Hanner, dated 19 April 1786, proved by Frederick Barfield; Ordered recorded.

Ordered Robert Wilkinson have an Order to build a Public Grist Mill on Bear Swamp on his own Plantation where he is the owner of the land on both sides of the Swamp & be allowed all benefits & priviledges allowed to persons who keep Public Grist Mills.

WEDNESDAY MORNING, Court met at 9 o'clock according to adjournment.

Present: Sam'l Houston, William Beck, John Lanier, Tho's Hooks, Fred'k Williams.

Bill of Sale: Richard Blackledge to Thomas Gray, bearing date 5 Nov. 1786, for sundry Negroes, a boy named Ben age about 15, a man named Dary age about 36, a lad named Aaron age about 18, two women named Bett & Nancy each about age 18, proved by Asher Pipkin; Ordered registered.

Bill of Sale: James Morris to William Beck, dated 25 Dec. 1786 for a Negro named Jack, Acknowledged; Ordered registered.

Bill of Sale: William Hurst to William Beck for a Negro named Lewis about 21, dated 24 Oct. 1786, proved by Samuel Slocumb; Ordered registered.

Ordered Frederick Barfield be Guardian to John Barfield & sell perishable Estate of said John Barfield & let the money arising therefrom on Interest for use of said John Barfield.

Granted petition of sundry persons, Inhabitants of this County, for an Order to lay off a Public Road from the North-East at Widow Barfields to join Charles Wards New Road near head of Rooty Branch or where most convenient.

Ordered Frederick Barfield, Anthony Jones, Edmund Duncan, Wm. Duncan, William Whitfield, Buckner Killegrew, Samuel Bowden, John Whitehead, Lewis Herring, Jacob Taylor, Demsey Westbrook, Stephen Jones, Samuel Rogers, William Wilkins & Edmund Duncan,Jr., or any twelve, be a Jury to lay off said Road & report to next Court.

Ordered Edmund Duncan,Jr., Constable, to summon & convene & James Outlaw to Qualify said Jury.

Last Will & Testament of Thomas Lanier proved by John Farrior; John Lanier & Benjamin Lanier Qualified as Executors.

Ordered Arthur, a Negro fellow of Estate of William Taylor, dec'd, continued as Miller to keep Mill belonging to said Estate, under direction of Katharin Taylor, the Admin'x of said Estate & he shall give due attendance at said Mill three days only in each week, Tuesdays, Thursdays & Saturdays & that he be exempted from doing all manner of Public Duties such as working on the Roads.

~~Ordered Kedar Bryan, Joseph Thomas Rhodes & Joseph Dickson be a Comm~~

James Kenan, one of Defendants Securities in suit of John Murphy vs. Ezekial Allen, surrendered Defendant to Court & is discharged.

Account of Sale of Estate of Demsey Canaday amounting to £232-9-4 rendered by William Lancaster; Ordered filed.

Settlement of Estate of Demsey Canaday, dec'd, Exhibited by William Lancaster & John Canaday, Ex'rs of said dec'd; Ordered filed.

Account current with Estate of Demsey Canaday, dec'd, Exhibited by William Lancaster, Ex'r, amounting to £106-7-2; Court concurred & Ordered filed.

Appointed Frederick Barfield constable for District of Capt. Outlaws Company; he gave Bond of £250 & took Oath of constable.

Appointed Edmund Duncan,Jr. constable for District of Capt. Bowdens Company; he gave Bond of £250 & took Oath of constable.

Ordered David Hall be Overseer of Road in room of Frederick Williams.

Account currant with Estate of Jesse Barfield, dec'd, Exhibited by Frederick Barfield, Admin'r; Court concurred & Ordered filed.

Receipt from Nathan Williams to Thomas James Exhibited: Received of Thomas James £120 in full of all Demands to this date, 18 July 1787, signed Nathan Williams; Ordered recorded.

Deed: James Kenan, Sheriff, to William Hunter for two pieces of land, Acknowledged; Ordered registered.

Deed: Elijah Bowen to Mesheck Stallins for 200 acres, proved by Shadrack Stallins; Ordered registered.

Deed: Mills Mumford to Thomas Shelton for 100 acres, proved by Anthony Jones; Ordered registered.

Deed: Joel Wilder to Jesse Brown for 120 acres, proved by William Farrior; Ordered registered.

Deed: Lewis Barnes to Bryan Whitfield for sundry pieces of land, proved by John Barfield; Ordered registered.

Deed: William O'Daniel to William Whitfield for 200 acres, proved by John Barfield; Ordered registered.

Deed: Theophilus Williams to James Morris for 100 acres, Acknowledged; Ordered registered.

Deed: David Cannon to James Morris for four pieces of land, 421 acres, proved by William Dickson; Ordered registered.

Deed: William Hunter to Andrew Laws for 200 acres, proved by Thomas Routledge; Ordered registered.

Deed: George Mallard to Daniel Mallard for 100 acres, proved by Phil Southerland; Ordered registered.

Deed: James Mills to William Hall for 100 acres, proved by Joseph Thomas Rhodes; Ordered registered.

Deed: David Greear to Stephen Miller for two pieces of land, proved by Charles Ward; Ordered registered.

Lease for lands from John Rhodes to Catharine Taylor, Acknowledged; Ordered registered.

Appointed Richard Cooper constable for District of Capt. Millers Company, he gave Bond of £250 & took Oath of Constable.

Whereas Abigal Brice, widow of Francis Brice, dec'd, had at last Term an Order passed in her favor to have 1/3 of land that did belong to Francis Brice as her Dower, which Order has not been executed for want of a Surveyor when Jury convened there; Ordered Sheriff to again convene a Jury upon premises to lay off & put said Abigal Brice in possession of 1/3 of said land as her Right of Dower & Ordered Sheriff to notice County Surveyor to attend said Jury & lay off said 1/3 of land.

THURSDAY MORNING, Court met at 9 o'clock according to adjournment.

Present: Worshipfull Tho. Routledge, Thomas Hooks, William Beck, Esquires.

Exempted Thomas Jernigan, aged & infirm man who is blind, from payment of a Poll Tax for himself in the future.

Ordered David Murdock, John Hill, Ephraim Garrison, Phil Southerland, James Maxwell, Robert Sloan, James Murrow, Benjamin Farrier, John Waller, Wm. Farrior, Temple Tillis, Auston Bryan, Mesheck Stallins, David Williams,Jr., Thomas Carleton, John Cook (IC), Jesse George, Jacob Teachy, Daniel Hicks, Alexander Wilson, James Wright, James Ward, Philip Ward, John Winder,Sr., John Cornegay, William Bizzel, Ruben Johnston, Owen O'Daniel, James Herring, Buckner Killigrew, James Taylor,Henry Houston, Lewis Barfield, William Mercer be Jurymen next Court.

Inventory of Estate of Nathaniel Love, an Idiot, Exhibited by James Kenan, his Guardian; Ordered registered.

Appointed Daniel Glisson constable in District of Capt. Kenans Company, he gave Bond of £250 & took Oath.

Appointed William Magee constable in District of Capt. Dicksons Company, he gave Bond of £250 & took Oath.

Ordered Frederick Graddy be Overseer of NorthEast Run or River from William Kornegays Landing up to Solomon Carters foot way in room of Samuel Sowell who is removed & have same Company of hands & that he proceed to work on said River or Run with said Company under direction of William Hubbard, James Outlaw & Frederick Barfield, a Committee appointed for that purpose.

Ordered Robert Twilly Overseer of Road in room of Henry Houston for ensueing year.

Jury appointed last Term to lay off a New Road from Pickets Landing on the NorthEast to end of New River Road at Onslow line, have laid off said Road & report: Beginning at James Pickets landing on NorthEast River from thence into Muddy Creek Road & from thence through Sarah Batts Plantation thence near an East Course to Onslow line at end of New Cut Road in Onslow County; Court concurred.

Daniel Glisson rendered his list of Insolvents on Taxable list of his District, amounting in the whole to £8-12-0 which Court allowed; Ordered Clerk to file same & furnish attested copy to enable him to settle with County Treasurer.

Auston Bryan, one of Collecters of Taxes, rendered a list of Insolvents amounting to £8-3-0 in money & £4-10-9 in tickets which Court allowed; Ordered recorded & filed & that said

Collecter be furnished with attested copy to enable him to settle with County Treasurer.

William Sulliven did give in three Negro Children as Taxables for 1786 which appears to be a mistake; Ordered Collecter remit to him amount of Taxes on said 3 Poll Taxables & Collecter be allowed same in his Insolvents for 1786.

James Pearsall, Esquire, produced a Commission from the Governor dated 18 July 1787, said Commission read & said James Pearsall gave Bond & Qualified & offered as Securities, in the Office of Sheriff, Alexander Dickson & Edward Dickson who were approved & entered into Bond of £5,000; James Pearsall offered also as Securities Alexander Dickson & Edward Dickson who were approved & entered into Bond of £10,000.

Whereas this Court granted an Order to Katharine Taylor appointing her Negro Fellow, Arthur, to be her Miller with a priviledge of being obliged to give attendance at said Mill only 3 days a week, which Court reconsidering are of opinion is contrary to Law; Ordered that as Mrs. Taylor have said Negro exempted from doing Public Duty, she shall cause her Negro to give due attendance according to Law.

John Matchet, one of the Collecters, rendered a list of Insolvents in his District amounting to £11-10-0, allowed by Court & Ordered filed; Attested copy delivered to said Collecter to enable him to settle with County Treasurer & others, said Collecter also returned John Baker a Poll Tax Supernumary by him collected.

Daniel Glisson, one of former Collecters, in a former settlement with Sheriff paid up General Tax in full before he had his Insolvents allowed, by which it now appears that said Glisson paid 42 shillings more than he collected; Ordered he be allowed said 42 shillings in his settlement with County Treasurer out of General Tax in his settlement for 1786 & Clerk certifie same.

Ordered Daniel Glisson, present Collecter, be allowed in his settlement in his Insolvents list for three Polls which were given in by Wm. Sullivent in a mistake which Court hath Ordered remitted to said William Sulliven by said Collecter.

Report of settlement between Auston Bryan & James Picket, heir of Thomas Picket, dec'd, Exhibited wherein there appears to be a Ballance due from Auston Bryan to said James Picket of £215-16-0; Court concurred & Ordered filed.

Inventory of Estate of Timothy Murphy, dec'd, Exhibited; Ordered filed.

Appointed Joseph Tho. Rhodes/Esq. to take list of Taxables in Capt. Southerlands Company.

Appointed Samuel Houston, Esq., to take list of Taxables in Capt. Houstons Company.

Appointed Thomas Routledge,Esq., take list of Taxables in Capt. Dicksons Company.

Appointed James Outlaw,Esq., to take list of Taxables in Capt. Outlaws Company.

Appointed Francis Olliver to take list of Taxables in Capt. Bowdens Company.

Appointed William Beck,Esq., to take list of Taxables in Capt. Kenans Company.

Appointed Fred'k Williams,Esq., to take list of Taxables in Capt. Stallins Company.

Appointed Daniel Teachy,Esq., to take list of Taxables in Capt. Teachys Company.

Appointed Charles Ward, Esq., to take list of Taxables in Capt. Millers Company.

Ordered each Justice, appointed to take list of Taxables in their several Districts, shall direct Constables in their District to notice Inhabitants to give in their lists & where no Constable is in the District, to Order & Authorize some person to summons the Inhabitants for that purpose.

Appointed Thomas Routledge Standard Keeper for this County & authorized him to purchase Sealed Weights & Measures, such as are necessary for that purpose & render his account for same to this Court.

Allowed Daniel Glisson 32 shillings for serving Court 4 days as Constable, to be paid out of County Tax.

Allowed William Magee 32 shillings for serving Court 4 days as Constable, to be paid out of County Tax.

Appointed Kedar Bryan & William Dickson to Inspect & take the Poll next Election for Representatives for this County.

Ordered Priam Pucket, Orphan about 12, bound Apprentice to Edward Dickson to learn to read & write.

Ordered Kedar Bryan, Joseph Dickson & Joseph Thomas Rhodes be a Committee to settle accounts of Estate of John Matchet, dec'd, between Ex'rs & Orphan of said dec'd, & report to next Court.

Deed: William Folsom to Phil Southerland [no amount], proved by William Southerland; Ordered registered.

Court Adjourned Till Court in Course.

[signed] Wm.Houston,Sr., Tho. Routledge, Joseph Dickson, Kedar Bryan, John Lanier, Thomas Hooks.

JULY TERM, 1787

Insolvents allowed Daniel Glisson for 1786:
Richard Henderson	1 Poll	£1- 1-0
James B[?]	1 Poll	1- 1-0
Miles Hutson	1 Poll	1- 1-0
Richard Singleton	1 Poll	1- 1-0
Robert Brock	1 Poll	1- 1-0
Elisha Carrol	1 Poll	1- 1-0
Thomas Jernigan	1 Poll	1- 1-0
William Sulliven	3 Polls	3- 3-0
John Rogers	1 Poll	-18-0
Daniel Ward, 100 acres		6-0
Also allowed Ballance of his Collection last year which he overpaid then		2- 2-0
The Whole		£13-16-0

Insolvents allowed Auston Bryan, Collecter for 1786:
Daniel Brown	1 Poll	£1- 1-0
John Little, 185 acres	1 Poll	1-15-0
John Moyan	1 Poll	1- 1-0
Joseph Moyan	1 Poll	1- 1-0
James Moyan	1 Poll	1- 1-0
William Harpe, 100 acres	1 Poll	1- 8-0
Peter Wood	1 Poll	1- 1-0
Jesse Brown	1 Poll	1- 1-0
Arthur Stokes, 200 acres		0-14-0
The Whole		£11- 3-0

Insolvents allowed John Matchet, Collecter for 1786:
Lewis Sowell	1 Poll	£1- 1-0
Rich'd Prescut, 75 acres	1 Poll	1-11-6
Ann Jones, Widow, 100 acres		0- 7-0
Joseph Moyan	1 Poll	1- 1-0
Lamuel Dunn	1 Poll	1- 1-0
Solomon Dobson, 210 acres	1 Poll	1-15-8
Matthew Gamey[?]	1 Poll	1- 1-0
John Barnhill	1 Poll	1- 1-0
Benja. Brock	1 Poll	1- 1-0
Lamuel Jones, 500 acres	1 Poll	1-15-0
The Whole		£11-15-2

15 October, 1787, County Court Begun & Held for County of Duplin at the Court House, the 3rd Monday.

Present: Worshipfull William Houston, Thomas Routledge, James Gillespie, John Lanier, Esquires.

Solomon Picket recorded his mark; ½ moon under right ear & a crop & hole in left.

TUESDAY MORNING, Court met at 9 o'clock according to adjournment.

Present: Worshipfull Wm. Houston, Tho. Routledge, Charles Ward, Samuel Houston, Esquires.

Bill of Sale: Thomas Gray to Elias James for a Negro woman, Nanny, Acknowledged; Ordered registered.

Inventory of Estate of Martha Shoaler, dec'd, Exhibited; Ordered filed.

Grand Jury sworn: John Hill, foreman, James Ward, John Kornegay, Buckner Killigrew, James Taylor, Owen O'Daniel, Henry Houston, Lewis Barfield, William Farrier, Auston Bryan, David Williams,Jr., Ephram Garrison, Phil Southerland, James Maxwell, Robert Sloan.

Ordered William Magee, Constable, attend Grand Jury.

Ordered William Shoaler have Admin'n on Estate of Martha Shoaler, dec'd; he offered as Security John Lanier & gave Bond of £100.

Granted petition of sundry Inhabitants of this County for a New Road from Soracta Town to Thomas Quins Plantation on the Newbern Road.

Ordered William Hubbard, Lewis Barfield, Anthony Miller, Loftis Worley, Edward Houston, Henry Houston, Wm. Mercer, Caleb Quin, Samuel Martindel, Stephen Martindill, Stephen Brady, Lott Gregory, Thomas Quin, Absalom Mercer, Joseph Canady be a Jury to lay off said Road. [evidently added to this Jury] R.Southerland, N.Fountain, John Waller,Jr., R. Bishop & ? .

Ordered William Ann Houston summon & convene & William Houston Qualify said Jury.

Ordered all Overseers of Roads in this County scited to return to next Court a list of hands in their Districts that Court may be better enabled to take proper orders thereon.

Post Inventory of Estate of William Taylor,dec'd, Exhibited by John Rhodes; Ordered filed.

Inventory of Estate of Thomas Lanier Exhibited by John Lanier, Admin'r; Ordered filed.

Exempted Hardy Benton,Sr., aged & infirm & having very little property, from paying Taxes as a Poll in the future.

Exempted Hardy Benton,Jr., very poor & Insane, from payment of Taxes in the future as a Poll.

Alexander Wilson, having been fined nisi at the last Court for not attending as a Juror last Term, Ordered discharged from said fine.

Ordered Frederick Barfield be Overseer of the New Road from Widow Barfields foard in NorthEast to New Road at head of Rooty Branch & have same hands which formerly did work under him.

As at October Court, 1786, Sampson Grimes was appointed Overseer of New Road on North side of Goshen Swamp & the hands named to work under him in said District & sundry of said hands have since been directed to work under Lavin Watkins, Overseer, Ordered Sampson Grimes be continued Overseer of said New Road & all said hands which were at first appointed to work under him be again added to his District & continue to work under him.

~~Thomas Hooks, Esquire, came before the Court & made complaint that Lewis Stuckey~~

Lewis Stuckey acknowledged himself justly indebted to State of North Carolina in the sum of £500 for keeping the peace with all persons, particularly with Thomas Hooks during the Term of 12 months & a day.

John Stuckey & Samuel Ward were also bound in the sum of £250 each in the manner as above as Securities for Lewis Stuckey.

Ordered James Ward be Overseer of the Road in room of James Winders & that Thomas Hooks,Sr. 4 [hands], Thomas Hills 4, Thomas Hooks,Jr. 1, Noel Penningtons 1, William Sullivens 2, Joseph Vicks 1 hand, Rich'd Singletons 1, John Hills 3, Edward Harris 3 hands work under him.

Bill of Sale: George Morrisay to James Pearsall for a Negro woman, Nanny, Acknowledged; Ordered registered.

WEDNESDAY MORNING, Court met at 9 o'clock according to adjournment.

Present: Worshipfull William Houston, Tho. Routledge, James Kenan, Robert Dickson, James Gillespie, John Lanier, Charles Ward, Samuel Houston, Esquires.

Bill of Sale: William Moore to Joseph Smith for a Negro woman, Silvia, proved by Isaac Hunter; Ordered registered.

Bill of Sale: Elizabeth Holingsworth to Jacob Hollingsworth for a Negro boy, Toney, proved by Joseph Thomas Rhodes; Ordered registered.

Joseph Thomas Rhodes, Esquire, returned his list of Taxables.

Daniel Teachy, Esquire, returned his list of Taxables.

James Outlaw, Esquire, returned his list of Taxables.

Francis Olliver, Esquire, returned his list of Taxables.

Granted Abraham Newton Admin'n on Estate of Jacob Newton, dec'd, he gave Bond of £200 & Qualified; Ordered him to sell Perishable Estate of said dec'd & report to next Court.

Ordered James Wright be Overseer of Road in room of Cullen Connerly & have same hands.

Samuel Houston, Esquire, returned his list of Taxables.

Deed: Samuel West to Elias James for 200 acres, proved by Charles James; Ordered registered.

Deed: Major Croom to James Gillespie for 100 acres, proved by Major Croom, Jr.; Ordered registered.

Deed: Robert Merrit to James Bland for 100 acres, proved by David Williams; Ordered registered.

Deed: Andrew Neely to James Bland for 100 acres, proved by Joshua Blanton; Ordered registered.

Deed: John Williams & his wife to Amos Johnston for 100 acres, proved by John Farrior; Ordered registered.

Deed: Thomas Phipps to Felix Frederick for 2 pieces land, proved by William Best; Ordered registered.

Deed: John Wright to Robert Byrd for 150 acres, proved by William Dickson; Ordered registered.

Deed: James Morris to Daniel Clarke for 421 acres, proved by Charles Brown; Ordered registered.

Deed: Samuel Bowden to Jesse Swinson for 160 acres, Acknowledged; Ordered registered.

Deed: James Kenan, Sheriff, to John Waller, Jr. for 100 acres, Acknowledged; Ordered registered.

Deed: John Rhodes to Henry, Penelope & Catharine McCulloh for sundry tracts, Acknowledged; Ordered registered.

Deed: Claudias Cartwright to John Blanton for 300 acres, proved by Joseph Dickson; Ordered registered.

Deed: Richard Meares to Patrick Newton for 2 pieces of land, proved by Austin Moore; Ordered registered.

Deed: William McGowen to James Gillespie for 6¼ acres, proved by Joseph Dickson; Ordered registered.

Deed: James Patterson & wife to James Gillespie for 232 acres, proved by Joseph Thomas Rhodes; Ordered registered.

Deed: Phill Southerland to William Southerland for 200 acres, Acknowledged; Ordered registered.

Deed: Abraham Newkirk to William Southerland for 280 acres, proved by Nathan'l McCann; Ordered registered.

Deed: William Taylor to Elisabeth Taylor, proved by John Gibbs; Ordered registered.

Deed: Jacob Mathews to John Matthews for 100 acres, proved by Joseph Wilson; Ordered registered.

Deed: Ebenezer Garrison to John Magee for 135 acres, proved by Wm. Farrior; Ordered registered.

Deed: Martin Wells to Nicholas Bryan for 2 pieces of land, proved by John Holden; Ordered registered.

Deed: James Wright & wife to Jacob Wells for 440 acres, proved by Daniel Teachy; Ordered registered.

Deed: Charles Hooten & wife to Lewis Thomas for 242 acres, proved by Deborah Phipps; Ordered registered.

Ordered David Murdock, Geo. Williams, Robert Williams,Jr., John Chambers, James McIntire, Alexander Dickson, James Midleton,Sr., James Evans, William Stokes, William McGowen, James Heath, Andrew Gufford, James Herring, Alexander Graddy, Jonathan Kitley, Edward Houston, Caleb Quinn, John Williams (BC), Robert Twilley, John Clarke, William Stevens, David Wright, Alex'r Wilson, William Guy, Felix Frederick, John Winders, William B[?], Rubin Johnston, John Shuffield, Britton Powell, William Bland, Thomas Carleton, Alexander Porter, William Ezel, Dan'l Southerland, William Hollingsworth, John Farior, Abraham Newkirk, Timothy Teachy, John Duff, Jacob Wells,Jr., Daniel Boney be Jury men to next Court.

Deed: James Pearsall,Sheriff, to James James for 100 acres, Acknowledged; Ordered registered.

Account of Division of Estate of William Taylor, dec'd, Exhibited by Committee; Court concurred & Ordered filed.

Upon motion of William McCann, Sr., Ordered Clerk bring to next Court Docket with Records of a Judgement which he formerly obtained against Henry & Henry Eustice McCulloh.

Robert Dickson, Admin'r of Isom Shuffield, dec'd, rendered account against Estate of said Isom Shuffield in which account the said Robert Dickson appears indebted to said Estate for £23-16-8; Court concurred & Ordered filed.

Granted James James a licence to keep a Tavern at his own house for one year, he offered as Securities Alexander Dickson & Daniel Glisson.

William Beck, Esq. returned his list of Taxables.

Ordered all hands & Overseers appointed to work on the NorthEast River & Goshen be discharged till next April from working on said River & Swamp & that they be considered liable to work on Roads as formerly.

Ordered James Gillespie, Sam'l Houston, Lewis Thomas & John Molten be Jury men to next Superior Court at Wilmington the 6th December next.

Ordered Robert Twilley & Anthony Miller, two Overseers of Road, with hands belonging to their Companies shall both jointly work on Soracta Bridge to middle of same till Bridge is finished.

Ordered William Korneguy be Overseer of New Road from middle of Main Run or River in Goshen Swamp out to Old Road near his Plantation & that his own hands & James Herrings hands, John Housman, Stephen Gufford, Jacob Glisson & Benjamin Herring work under him.

Ordered Stephen Miller be Overseer of New Road on South side of Goshen from middle of Main Run or River in Goshen Swamp to Old Road near Archibald Carrs & that George Millers hands, John Chambers hands, James Chambers hands, William Coles hands, Clem't Godfrey, Jerediah Bass Foley, Flud Foley work under him on said Road.

Deed: Thomas Baker to John Magee for 100 acres, proved by William Farrier; Ordered registered.

Frederick Williams, Esq. returned his list of Taxables.

Arthur Stokes, Admin'r of Philip Rouse, dec'd, rendered a further account against the Estate of said dec'd, amounting to £1-18-8; Court concurred & Ordered filed.

Ordered Executors of John Matchet, dec'd, scited to next Court to render account of their Executorship.

Ordered William Ann Houston be constable in District of Capt. Houstons Company, he gave Bond & Qualified.

Ordered Alexander Dickson be Overseer in room of Thomas Johnston the ensuing year.

Appointed Justus Miller constable for District of Capt. Southerlands Company, he gave Bond & Qualified.

Account current with Estate of John Matchet, dec'd, Exhibited by Sarah Matchet, widow of said Matchet, amounting to £77-17-4; Court concurred & Ordered filed; Ordered also that Executors of Will of said Matchet pay said Sarah Matchet the above sum of £77-17-4 out of moneys & Perishable part of Estate after deducting such sums as she may owe said Estate for purchases made by her at sale thereof.

Ordered Tavern Keepers shall observe the following rates:

Dinner, 2 or more Dishes & Grog or Cider	£0-3-6
Dinner without Grog or Cider	2-0
Dinner, cold victuals	1-6
Supper in same manner, same prices	1-6
Breakfast, with Coffee or Tea	2-0
Breakfast, with cold meat or milk	1-0
Lodging, a good Clean bed, each person	0-6
Grog or Tody of West India Rum, p Quart	2-0
Do, Good Brandy, p Quart	2-0
Good Summer Cyder, p Quart	0-6
Crab or Seedling Cyder, after October	1-0
Taffey Rum, p Gill	0-4
Indian Corn, p Quart	0-4
Stableage p Night without fodder or Hay	1-6
Good Pasturage p Night	0-6
Best West India Rum, p Quart	4-0
West India Rum, p Gill	0-10
Good Brandy, p Quart	4-0
Good Brandy, p Gill	0-10
Taffey Rum, p Quart	2-0
W't Indian Rum when drank on the Plantation, p Quart	5-4

Granted Edward Houston licence to keep a Tavern at his own house at Soracta; Ordered Clerk to take his Bond.

Appointed Auston Bryan Collector for District of Capt. Dicksons, Capt. Stallins, Capt. Teacheys & Capt. Southerlands Companies; Ordered he give Bond.

Appointed Daniel Glisson Collector of all Taxes in Districts of Capt. Kenans & Capt. Bowdens Companies; Ordered he give Bond at next Court.

Appointed Frederick Barfield Collector of Taxes in District of Capt. Outlaws, Capt. Houstons & Capt. Millers Companies; Ordered he give Bond at next Court.

Granted Theophilus Williams a Licence to keep a Tavern at his own house at Goshen; Ordered Clerk to take his Bond.

Ordered Scitations issued to following persons to bring to next Court the Orphans in their families:
Ann Bowen, one daughter
Eve Boney, one son
Aly Taylor, one daughter
Prudence Taylor, one daughter
Sarah Williams, one son
Elisabeth Eayers, one daughter, two sons
Widow Bralchers Children
Margaret Pickets Children
Widow Parker, Children
Widow Harrill, Children
Caty Dunn, Children
Hannah Batts, Children.

Ordered Adam Run[?] & Thomas Miller, two aged & infirm men having very little property, exempted from paying Taxes as Poll Taxables for future.

Charles Ward, Esq. returned his list of Taxables.

Allowed William Magee 24 shillings for attending Court as Constable three days this Term.

Allowed Daniel Glisson 32 shillings for attending Court as Constable four days this Term.

Allowed Thomas Quin 16 shillings for attending Court as Constable two days this Term.

Court Adjourned Till Court in Course.

[signed] Tho. Routledge, Robert Dickson, Cha. Ward, James Gillespie, Joseph Dickson.

INDEX

AARON
   John 26
ADAMS
   Andrew 3
ALBERSON (Albertson)
   John 46
   Samuel 4,17,46
   Sarah 77
   William 17
ALDERMAN (Aulderman)
   Daniel 31,32,38,70
   David 31,38,70
   John 38
ALLEN
   Ezekiel 44,87
   Henry 56,66
   Isabel 55
   John 55
   Nancy 55
   Peggy 55
   Sarah 34
   William 18,34,44,65
ALPIN
   David 50
ANDERSON
   William 70
ANDREWS
   Abraham 29,30,80
ARMSTRONG
   Alexander 8
   Edward 4
   John 4,21,62,71,83,85
ASHE
   Samuel,Jr. 45
ATKINS
   John 69,77
   Samuel 66
ATKINSON
   John 24
   Mary 24
   Thomas 24
AVERS
   John 20,72
BACK SWAMP 80
BAILY
   Anthony 66
   Jones 75
BAKER
   John 90
   Jonathan 81
   Thomas 97
BALL
   William 23

BALLARD
   Plunket 1
BARBREE
   Peggy 22
   Peter 22
BARFIELD (Bearfield)
   Captain 3
   Frederick 2,3,10,20,24,30,
     34,36,39,42,45,47,51,52,
     54,56,61,77,78,81,86,87,
     89,94,98
   Jesse 76,77,87
   John 86,88
   Lewis 67,83,89,93
   Stephen (Steven) 11,39,40,
     56,60
   Widow 87
BARFIELDS FOARD 94
BARNES (Barns, Bames)
   Lewis 7,18,19,25,62,67,68,88
BARNHILL
   John 92
BASS
   Andrew 38
   Willis 31
BATTS
   Hannah 34,99
   Sarah 34,89
BEAR SWAMP 5,46,86
BECK
   Christopher 66
   John 4-8,17,22-24,28,38,
     43-45,52-54,56,61,62,83
   John,Jr. 27
   Stephen 27,56
   William 7,8,10,27,47,56,62,
     68,78,83,86,89,91,97
BEESLEY
   Abraham 29,30
   Auston 29,62,71
   Solomon 8,29,36,37,62,65,
     66,71,75
BENNET
   Samuel 27
   Thomas 27,39,83,85
   William 27
BENTON
   Hardy,Jr. 49,94
   Hardy,Sr. 49,94
   Josiah 49
   Samuel 49

BEST
   Benjamin 26,55,78
   Howell 26
   John,Jr. 26
   John,Sr. 19,26,63
   William 2,4,5,7,10,13,14
     19,23,28,76,95
BEVEN
   Joseph 16,22,30
   Joseph,Jr. 16,38
   Joseph,Sr. 20,33,38
   William 16,33,38,66
BEVERIT
   Jacob 22
BINS CREEK 38
BISHOP
   Robert 36,65,68,81,93
BIZZEL (Bizzell)
   Arthur 1,27,40
   Hardy 27
   James 1,4,14,27,36
   William 36,89
BLACKLEDGE
   Richard 86
BLACKMAN
   Joab 13,15
   Stephen 44
BLACKMORE
   Edward 2
   Herald 2,7,20
BLACKSHIRE
   Moses 37
BLACK SWAMP 73
BLAKE
   Joshua 39
BLAND (Blann)
   James 25,38,95
   William 38,96
BLANTON
   James 38
   John 8,70,96
   Joshua 38,95
BLIZZARD
   Hezekiah 3
BLOODWORTH
   Timothy 30
BLOUNT
   Benjamin 27,70
   Warrin 15,27,32,33,37,41
     43,45,71
BONEY
   Daniel 56,96
   Eve 99
   Jacob 45-47
   John 7,10,60,72,75,78
   Wimbert 16,29,59,83

BOSTICK
   Charles 65,68
BOWDEN
   Baker 27,40
   Captain 3,10,12,34,42,54,
     57,63,64,84,87,91,98
   Nicholas 27,36,47,82,84
   Samuel 4,20,26,40,54,63,75,
     76,79,83,85,87,95
   Samuel,Jr. 27
BOWEN (Bowing)
   Aaron 38
   Ann 99
   Ann Phillis 17
   Clifton 8
   Daniel 38,70
   Elijah 1,8,17,33,38,40,46,
     59,70,88
   Stephen 39
BOWENS FOARD 33
BOWZER
   Emanuel 29,67
BOYD
   Samuel 20
   William 5
BOYET
   Absalom 79
   William 46
BRADLEY (Bradly)
   James 27
   John 10,27,47,82,83
   John,Jr. 36
   Richard 4,27,54,63,75,76
   Thomas 63,75
BRADY
   Stephen 60,93
BRALCHER
   Widow 99
BRANCH
   Burwell 75
   Dred 27
   Jesse 75
   Moses 27,38
BRAY
   Joseph 25,35,70
   Joseph,Sr. 36,66
BRICE
   Abigal 55,78,88
   Francis 78,88
BRIDGE TOLLS 13,14
BRINSON
   Charlotte 11
   Vialator 11

BROCK
  Barnet 68,75
  Benja 92
  Besent 25,26,81
  Jesse 18,26,54,63
  John 19,26,51
  Lewis 22,83
  Robert 92
BROCKS LANDING 80
BROOKS LANDING (Brocks?) 81
BROWN
  Charles 10,26,56,63,69,95
  Daniel 92
  Jacob 10
  Jesse 4,46,61,73,77,80,88,92
  John 39
BRUINGTON
  Sarah 43
BRYAN (Briant)
  Austin (Auston) 36,47,62,63,66,69,71,89,90-93,98
  John 21
  Kedar (Kader) 5,10,11,15-17,19,21-23,31-34 42-45,48,52-55,57,61-64,71,75,78,80,87,91
  Nicholas 8,96
  Rebecca 9
BUCK
  John 44
BUCK SWAMP 28
BUIE
  Francis 72
BULLARD
  Nathan 26
  William 63
BULLS
  Henry 70
BULL TAIL BRANCH 16,33,38 47,66,68
BUNTING
  David 17,19,39,85
BURDOO
  March'l 20
BURNHAM (Burnam)
  William 6,10,27,41
BURNCOAT 5,19,28,29,46 56,60,83,96
BURRIS
  Priscilla 34
BURTON
  Thomas 46
  Watson 2,10,19,61
  William 4,38,61

BUTLER
  John 16,50
BYRD
  Daniel 27
  Micajah 27
  Robert 95
  Robert,Jr. 27
  Shadrick 27
  Sutton 6
CADE
  Catharin 79
  Patience 5,7
  Stephen 3,5,7,20,79
CAMPBELL
  William 78,80
CANADAY (Canady)
  Demsey 84,87
  John 87
  Joseph 93
  Thomas 20,81
CANNON
  David 10,11,26,27,32,36 40,48,82,88
  David,Jr. 4,14,29,63
  Dennis 11
CANNONS SLEW 27,48,82
CARLETON
  John 39,52,62
  Peter 4
  Thomas 7,13,17,20,21,36 62,71,89,96
CARMAN
  Samuel 50
CARR
  Archibald 10,54,63,67, 72,75,97
  Barbara 5,6,18
  James 29,32,40,41,43,58 70,71
  John 4,14,15,40
  Joseph 5,18
  William 6,7,10,18,40,56, 60,68,83
CARROL (Carroll)
  Elisha 7,92
  Hardy 30
  John 22
  Thomas 31
CARTER
  Davie 3
  Edward 18
  Edward John James Augustus 35
  John James E.Augustus 60
  Silas 4,63
  Solomon 3,18,25,35,78,81,89

CARTERS FOOTWAY 21,81,89
CARTERS MILL 39
CARTRIGHT
  Claudius 50,96
  Joseph 38
CASWELL
  Richard, Gov. 23,68
CENSUS 41,44,45
CHAMBERS
  James 25,35,97
  John 4,14,25,72,75,96,97
CHAMBERS FOARD 25
CHAMBLES
  Joshua 26,63
CHANCE
  Asa 54
CHASTEN (Chasen)
  Richard 19,72,75
CHERRY
  Willis 27,41,43,48,
    65,68,82
CHUBBUCK
  Jeremiah 39
CLARK (Clarke)
  Daniel 27,41,83,95
  James 27
  John 27,47,56,61,96
  Thomas 79
CLINTON
  Richard 4,18,44
COCKE
  John 74
COCKER
  Dr. 69,77
COCKERS LAND 45
COGGIN
  Ruth 34
COLE
  Robert 73,80
  William 86,97
CONNER
  James 76
  Moses 25
CONNERLY (Conolly)
  Cullen 5,27,36,82,95
COOK
  John 20,29,32,46,65,
    68,69,71,89
  Rubin 27
COOKS MILL 62,71
COOPER
  George 34,63,78,83
  George,Jr. 26,60
  George,Sr. 26,60,63,85
  John 78
  Richard 20,22,26,63,85,88

COPPERSMITH
  Virginia 21
COTTLE
  Robert 73
COX
  James 20,80
  Jasper 31
  John 29,32,36
  Joseph,Jr. 71
  Joseph 8
  Solomon 20
COXWELL
  Benjamin 8
CRANFORD
  John 39
CREAMER
  Mary Ann 54
CROOM
  Major 29,95
  Major,Jr. 95
CROSS ROADS 1,12,62,71
CROSSING
  Thomas 38,39,50,53
CRUMPTON
  Thomas 4,16,33,35,39
CURTIS
  William 77
CYPRESS CREEK 41,45,69,77
DANIEL
  Aaron 27
  Hardy 27
  Jephtha 27
  John,Jr. 27
  Shadrick 10,27
DAVIS
  Absalom 37
  David 25,29,38,41,70
  Jonathan 29
  Samuel 38
  Shaderick [?] 10
  Simon 78
  Windell 46
DAVISON (Davidson)
  Isaac 3
  Joseph 9
DAWSON
  Benjamin 84,85
  Isaac 78
DEBRUEL (Debruhl,Dibruhl)
  Edward Cornwallis 9,36,70,78
  Mary 70
DEVER
  John 40
DICKSON
  Alexander 4,15,39,47,58,
    58,62,65,71,74,90,96-98

DICKSON (continued)
  Captain 3,63,89,91,98
  Edward 4,10,14,16,25,33-36
    38,40,47,62,66,68,71,80,
    83,90,91
  James 4,7,10,19,20,22,28,
    29,31,36,40,59,65,68,
    71,72,83
  Joseph 1-3,5-9,11-15,17,19-23
    28-31,33-35,37,40-43,45-49,
    51-57,59,61-64,67,68,70-74,
    76,78,80,84,87,91,96,99
  Michael 30
  Robert 1,5,9,15,17-21,23-31,
    33-35,37,40,41,47,49,51-55,
    57-59,61-69,71-73,75,78,80,
    81,86,94,97,99
  William 5,8,9,13,15,17-19,23,
    27,28,30,36,38,42,47,56,59,
    70,72-74,76,79,83,84,86,88,
    91,95
DOBBS COUNTY 46,76.
DOBSON
  Solomon 24,92
  William 23,32
DUFF
  John 30,45,79,96
  William 16
DULANY (Dulaney)
  Benjamin 19,79
DUNCAN (Dunkin)
  Edmond 54,87
  Edmund,Jr. 54,64,87
  Edmond,Sr. 64
  Isaac 64
  William 29,32,35,54,64,87
DUNN
  Caty 99
  Lamuel 92
  Lemon 26,51
DURRELL
  John 35
EASOM
  John 9
EAYERS
  Elisabeth 99
EDWARDS
  Joshua 33,38
  Nathaniel 29,33,74
  William 61
ELKINS
  Samuel 39
ELLIOT
  Elizabeth 2
ELLIS
  James 56

ELLISSA
  James 8
ENNIS
  David 38
ENZOR
  Ambrose 39,59
EVANS (Evins,Evens)
  James, 4,9,10,12,28,29,
    32,46,68,96
  John 71
EZEL
  Benjamin 6,27,60
  William 96
FAISON
  Henry 8,27,62
  James 8
  Kilby 11
FARRIER (Farrior,Farior)
  Benjamin 89
  John 3,4,15,18,43,73,
    87,95,96
  William 3,73,83,88,89,
    93,96,97
FENNELL (Fennel)
  Nicholas 20,29,30,50
FLANAGAN
  Tebtha 41
FLEMING
  James 26
  John 26,63
FLOWERS
  Simon 27
  Thomas 10,27,29,56,60,65
  William 8
FOLEY
  Elizabeth 25
  Flud 25,51,97
  Jerediah Bass 97
  Jeremiah 25
  John 40
FOLEYS SLEW 27,28
FORT
  John 8
FOLSOM
  William 91
FOUNTAIN
  Captain 3
  Henry 20,73,80
  Joab 29
  Nathan 20,29,32,41,56
    61,73,80,93
FRAZAR
  Dr. 27
  James 27
  Micajah 27

FREDERICK
  Felix 5,27,40,47
    53,80,95,96
  William 5,19,20,28,40,
    41,43,72,75,76,85
FUSSELL
  Benjamin 79
  Eliza 46
  Jacob 30
FUSSELLS CREEK 16,25
GAINEY (Ganey)
  Matthew 26,51,92
  William 4,18
GARRISON
  Adonijah 1,9,36,37,59
  Ebenezer 3,20,81,96
  Ephram 1,19,20,22,36,83,
    89,93
GARRISS
  Bukford 64
GAVIN
  Thomas 39
GAVINS OLD FOARD 26
GAVINS SLEW 26
GAYLOR
  George 27
GEORGE
  David 61
  Jesse 4,10,36,46,66,89
GEORGIA 4
GIBBS
  Elisha 27
  John 36,39,79,96
  John,Jr. 27
GILLESPIE
  Borthrik 37,42
  Captain 10,12,31,34,
    42,57,58,64
  James 2,3,5,6,13-16,18-21,
    23,28,30-32,34-37,40-42,
    52-55,57-61,65-68,71-74,
    80,84,93-97,99
GLISSON
  Abraham 10,35,40
  Daniel 7,9,10,12,22,27,29,
    36,41,45,48,57,58,63,67,
    76,82,83,89,90,92,97-99
  Frederick 18
  Jacob 4,26,41,43,97
  John 4,26,72
  Michael 5,20,21,23,46,47,
    53,62
GODFREY
  Clement 19,25,97

GODWIN
  Jacob 13,15
  Joseph 21
  Nathan 9
GOFF
  Charles 20,22
  Demsey 26
  John 83,85
  John,Jr. 33,41,43,72
  John,Sr. 16,33,38
  William 17,23,25,33,52
GOODING
  George 50
Goodman
  Henry 39,76
  James 6,49
  Solomon 17
GOSHEN SWAMP 5,9,10,14,17,19,
  20,25,28,47,48,53,54,62-65,
  67,77,81-83,94,97,98
GOW
  John 29
GRADDY
  Alexander 7,10,65,67,68,78,96
  Frederick 15,24,56,67,76-78,
    81,83,85,89
  John 77,85
  Lewis 30
  William 18,20,41,78
  William,Sr. 56,60
GRANT
  Jesse 27
GRAY
  Alex'r 43
  Elizabeth,Mrs. 32
  James 20
  John 32
  Mr. 66,80
  Thomas 5,7-10,17,18,20,23,
    24,27,28,38,40,43,55,
    84-86,93
GREEAR
  David 19,25,35,36,88
GREEN
  James 7,32
  John 79
  Lott 35
  Rubin 35,38,50
  Thomas 79
GREGORY
  Lott 4,29,93
GRIFFIN
  John 27

GRIMES
    James 26,45,54,63,68
    Joseph 4,5,12-14,17,19
        26,28,39,45-48,60,62,
        63,69,71,72,77,81,82
    Sampson 26,36,46,48,63,
        82,83,85,94
GRIMES MILL 61
GRIMES SLEW 82
GROVE ACADEMY 72
GROVE BRIDGE 5,12,15,19,
    28,46,63,65,67,68,77
GROVE SWAMP 6
GUFFORD
    Andrew 26,30,40,65,68,96
    James 26,40
    Stephen 8,19,26,29,32,41,
        43,46,97
GULLY
    William 10,17,27
GURGANUS
    Uriah 26,48,63,81
GUY
    James 26
    Samuel 5,20
    William 5,12,13,27,47,96
HAGAN
    Rachel 7
HAINES
    John 10,27,56
HALL
    David 35,87
    Drury 3,4,56
    James 56
    Patience 7
    Peter 19,24,51
    Philip 7
    William 4,5,9,13,19,28,29
        36,42,72,77,88
HALSO
    John 8
HAMBLETON
    Elizabeth 6,9
HANCHY
    Martin 20
    Moses 20,29,39
HARPE
    William 92
HARRELL
    Cader 18
    James 27
    Widow 99

HARRIS
    Cason 63
    Edward 7,26,61,94
    John 60
    William 11,29,64
HART
    John 27
HATCHER
    Hancock 2,20,40
HAWTHORN
    William 81
HAY
    John 61
HAYWOOD
    George 69
HEATH
    James 8,20,29,96
    Thomas 4,29,72,75
HEDGEMAN
    George 11
    Lewis 11
HENDERSON
    Ann 34
    Anna 52
    James 57
    Lucy 57
    Richard 92
    Sarah 57
HERRING
    Alexander 26
    Arthur 15,19,20,24,25
    Arthur,Jr. 26
    Benjamin 2,26,67,72,75,97
    Daniel 2,5,11,17,19,20,
        26,28,48
    James 8,81,89,96,97
    John 35
    Joseph 34,41,44
    Lewis 87
    Stephen 11,19,20,26,29,
        44,48,63,81
    Stephen,Jr. 27
    Whitfield 26
HERRINGS SLEW 26
HICKS
    Daniel 2,4,11,20,21,29,36,
        40,42,44,83,89
    Thankful 6,21,23
HILL
    John 7,14,20,22,26,41,43,46,
        47,52,83,89,93,94
    Thomas 4-6,14,17,18,22,26,
        38,56,61,72,75,94
    William Henry 85
HILLS FOARD 26

HINES
  Isaac 60
  Lewis 1,21,23,25,29,
    32,37,60,81
  William 64,69
HODGESON
  Aaron 25
  Joseph 25
HOGANS
  Rachel 32
HOGG & CAMPBELL 69
HOGG
  Robert 64
HOLDEN
  John 70,79,96
HOLLAND
  Henry 7
  James 23
HOLLINGSWORTH
  Elisabeth 95
  Henry 24,30
  James 20
  Jacob 20,95
  William 17,36,43,56,61,
    73,80,86,96
  Zeb 50
HOMES
  Fred'k 27
  George 55
HOOKS
  Charles 26
  Hillary 27,47,65,68,83
  Thomas 3,5,7,17-19,28,
    36,38,44-46,53,54,63,
    65,67-69,71,76,78,80,
    82,86,89,91,94
  Thomas,Jr. 26,82,94
  Thomas,Sr. 26,94
  William 4,14,15,26,36,82
HOOTEN
  Charles 96
HOUSMAN
  Captain 3
  John 4,5,14,19,25,54,67,
    70,71,77,97
  Stephen 11
HOUSTON
  Captain 3,63,84,90,97,98
  Dr. 19,25,81
  Edward 19,25,36,47,53,56,
    67,81,84,93,96,98
  Henry 7,10,36,89,93
  Samuel 1,3,7,12,19,21,23,
    24,31,34,36,38,40,42,43,
    45,47,52-59,61,64,65,67,
    69,75,76,78,80,81,84,86
    90,93-95,97

HOUSTON (continued)
  William 12,23,24,28-30,
    33,35,45,47,52-56,61,
    67,68,71,74,76,78,80,
    93,94
  William,Sr. 1,9,11,12,31,
    37,48,58,73,84,91
  William Ann 93,97
HOWARD
  Samuel 12
HUBBARD
  Captain 2,10,12,34,42,
    57,64
  William 20,22,23,39,47,67,
    71,72,77,81,83,84,89,93
HULET
  Jeremiah 78
HUMPHRY
  John 65
HUNTER
  Isaac 2,5,19,24,28,34,47,
    74,77,80,95
  Nicholas 2,5,8,12,15,19,
    23,28,36,47,53,69,83,85
  William 88
HURST
  Isaac 22
  James,Jr. 79
  William 6,7,9,10,22,27
    45,86
HURSTS BRIDGE 5,17
HUSKE
  John 64,69
HUTSON
  Joseph 38,69
  Miles 92
INDIAN GRAVES 20,80
INDICO BRANCH 62
ISLAND CREEK 20,89
IVEY
  Curtis 14
  Robert 59
JACKSON
  James 28
JAMES
  Charles 4,16,25,35,95
  Elias 16,20,25,93,95
  James 1,2,9,29,38,39,46,
    53,57,58,96,97
  Joel 15
  John 46
  Thomas 3,4,14,15,29,32,40,
    62,65,71,72,88
  William 79

- 107 -

JERNIGAN
   Elisha 27,33,36,45,
      47,53,84
   Thomas 24,26,89,92
JOHNS
   Isabel 46
JOHNSTON (Johnson)
   Amos 95
   Benja 20,21,22,72
   Hanch 70
   John 10,25,46,67,70
   John,Jr. 9,29,32
   Joseph 4,9,45,71
   Rubin 11,29,32,54,
      64,89,96
   Sasaby [?] 39
   Thomas 42,98
JONES
   Abe 43
   Ann, Widow 92
   Anthony 18,25,54,56,60,
      87,88
   Elisha 6,64
   Henry 44,51,61
   Lamuel 92
   Lewis 55,64,69
   Samson 52
   Samuel 23,61,68
   Samuel,Jr. 19,25,84
   Stephen (Steven) 40,87
   Widow 55
   William 33
KENAN
   Captain 3,10,12,34,42,
      57,63,64,84,89,91,98
   Colonel 22
   Felix 18,20,22,33,34,
      37,41,44
   James, Colonel 1
   James 5-9,12,15,18,19,
      21,23,28,43,46,52,53,
      55,72,73,84,87-89,
      94,95
   Michael J. 79
   Michael T. 9,11
   William 2,4-6,10,13,14,
      22,24,26,34,37,41,44,
      46,56,60,63,71,80
KILLIGREW
   Buckner 45,55,62,87,89,93
KILLIT
   Andrew 9
KING
   Lavin 86
   Stephen 15
   Tabitha 39

KINNARD (Kinard)
   Michael 62,72
   Nathaniel 6,10,27,41
KINNARDS BRIDGE 28
KITLEY
   John 4
   Jonathan 4,55,58,96
KNIGHT
   William 46
KNOWLES
   James 16,25,35
   John 66
   William 35
KORNEGAY (Kernegay, Cornegay)
   Abraham 30
   George 54,72,75
   George, Jr. 4,64
   Jacob 35,40,75
   John 35,54,63,64,89,93
   William 19,20,22,24,25,41,
      43,65,67,68,72,77,81,89,97
KORNEGAYS BRIDGE 19,20,24,25,
   68,77,81
KORNEGAYS LANDING 89
LAINE
   Alexander 6,24,34,39
   Alexander,Jr. 39
LAITON
   William 21,31,33
LAM
   Gillispie 20
LANCASTER
   William 87
LANGSTON
   Absalam 1
LANIER
   Alexander 41
   Benjamin 6,20,56,87
   Benjamin, Jr. 4
   Bird 32
   James 20
   Jesse 72,75,80
   John 20,22,41,56,65,68,69,
      73,76,77,80,84-87,91,93,94
   Lamuel 73
   Thomas 87,94
LASSITER
   George 9
LAWHAN
   Elisabeth 76
LAWS
   Andrew 88
LEE
   Joshua 31,50
LESTER
   Robert 78

LIMESTONE CREEK 6,12,13,19
  42,44,66
LITTLE
  John 38,60,92
  Joseph 39
LOCKHART
  Elizabeth 43
  James 2,7,8,12,13,18,
    22-24,34,37,40,43,
    53,59,60,71
LOCKHARTS MILL 61
LOVE
  James 56
  Loughlin 14,16,29
  Nathaniel 65,72,89
LYNOUGH
  Ealse 61,63
  Eulee 42
  Francis 37,42,61,63
McCALLOP
  Daniel 32
  John 27
McCANN
  Hugh 5,18
  Hugh,Jr. 25
  Nathaniel 19,20,25,
    80,83,85,96
  Nothial 10
  Patrick 27
  William 20,65
  William,Sr. 97
  William,Jr. 25,65
McCARTY
  Florance 66
McCLAM
  William 13,15,16,21,23,
    31,33
McCULLOH
  Catharin 38,95
  Henry 38,95,97
  Henry Eustice 9,24,34,
    41,44,45,71,97
  James 18,38,44,75
  John,Jr. 65,68
  Penelope 38,95
McGEE (see Magee)
  William 12
McGOWEN
  William 2,5,19,28,36,
    37,42,44,58,64-66,
    68,96
McINTIRE
  Deny 20
  Derry 81
  James 2,5,12,19,28-31,
    47,56,61,66,83,96

MAGEE
  John 3,18,20,55,57,96,97
  William 2,3,6,13,18,19,21,
    28,41,42,53,57,58,61,62,
    66,67,72,75,83,85,89,91,
    93,99
MAINER
  Jacob 81
  Jethro 26
  John 25,26,63,81
  Solomon 33
  William 26
MALLARD
  Daniel 88
  George 20,22,29,88
  John 19,41,43,56
MANNING
  Martha 54
  Moses 3
MARCUS
  Absalom 22
MARSH BRANCH 36
MARTIN
  Aaron 28
  Christopher 16,26,40,63,78,80
MARTINDEL
  Samuel 93
  Stephen,Sr. 65
MATCHET
  John 4,7,9,10,19,25,28,32,
    36,47,48,53,57,63,65,67,
    72,81,82,90-92,97,98
  Sarah 4,98
  William 4,28
MATCHETS SLEW 26
MATHIS (Mathews,Matthews)
  Arthur 6,30,39,62,71
  Edmund 4,18
  Jacob 4,15,39,46,62,71,96
  James 20,25,36,37,81
  John 71,84,96
  Mary 6
  Rice 34,79
  Rich'd 23
MAXWELL
  David 68,85
  James 5,16,18,19,30,39,68,
    72,85,89,93
MAXWELL SWAMP 15
MEARS
  Richard 4,14,26,42,96
MERCER
  Absalom 20,76,93
  William 89,93
MERCHANT
  John 59

- 109 -

MERRIT
   Charles 6,60
   Robert 30,70,95
   William 4,14,46
MIDLETON
   David 6
   Isaac 4
   James 7,10,12,19,
     20,32,42,47,65
   James,Sr. 4,5,11,
     19-22,28,41,43,
     71,74,96
   James,Jr. 5,28,29,
     41,86
   William 2
MILLARD
   Hezekiah 27
   Isaac 3,27
   Jacob 27
MILLER
   Anthony 19,20,22,
     25,43,72,81,93,97
   Captain 3,10,34,42,
     57,63,88,91,98
   Charles 19,25,65
   George 5,17,20,28,
     81,82,97
   Justus 98
   Mary 65
   Stephen 10,19,25,29,
     32,36,47,48,52,57,
     65,81,83,88,97
   Thomas 99
MILLERS FOARD 25
MILLERS LAGOON 81
MILLS
   Cato 20
   Hicks 79
   James 4,14,15,19,23,
     41,64,88
   Leonard 20
   Mingo 20
   Rawley 8,22
MOLTEN
   Abraham 5,62,71
   Abraham,Jr. 43,76
   John 2,5,7,11,20-22,
     56,58,61,62,65,71,
     80,85,97
MONK
   Jacob 27
MOORE
   Austin 70,96
   Betsey 2
   James 15,18,27,49
   John 2,5,8,15

MOORE (continued)
   Maurice 2
   Orson 5
   William 5,15,34,40,95
MORGAN
   Joseph 56
MORRISS
   James 11,36,41,47,72,84,
     86,88,95
MORRISAY
   George 94
MORROW
   John 79
MOUNS [?]
   Richard 46
MOYAN
   James 92
   John 92
   Joseph 92
MUDDY CREEK 61,73,80,89
MULDROUGH
   John M. 4
MUMFORD
   Mills 25,36,88
MUNDS
   Richard 18,20
MURDOCK
   David 32,36,63,65,68,89,96
MURPHY
   John 14,87
   Timothy 7,25,29,33,35,77,84,
   William 33,41,43
MURRAY
   James 20,41,72,75,80
   James,Sr. 70,76
   James,Jr. 70,81
MURROW
   James 24,89
   John 75
   Widow 25
NAHUNGA 5,36,46
NEALE
   John 4,15,67,68,78
   John,Sr. 65
   John,Jr. 4,19,25,81
NEELEY
   Andrew 30,50,95
NETHERCUT
   William 4,14,18,56,60,68
   William,Sr. 56,65
   William,Jr. 60,81
NEW
   John 19,25
   Margaret 7
   William 20,81

NEWBERN 72,93
NEWELL
  Nathan 70
  Peter 16
NEW HANOVER COUNTY 33,46
NEWKIRK
  Abraham 20,55,56,66,
    68,71,75,81,86,96
  Henry 20,29,30,32,
    47,53,56,81
NEWTON
  Abraham 33,38,60,70,95
  Isaac 38,72
  Jacob 38,95
  James 70
  John 2,27,61
  Joshua 70
  Lois 60,70
  Patrick 2,26,56,70,
    71,72,75,96
  Sarah 50
  Suckey 52,53
  William 4,5,14,15,27,61
NORRIS
  Jesse 20
  Patrick 22
NORTH EAST RIVER 13,19,20,
  24,25,28,39,42,44,46,54-56,
  58,63-68,77,80,81,83,86,87,
  89,94,97
OATES
  James 10,27
O'DANIEL
  Owen 3,11,45,48,65,68,
    76,81,83,89,93
  William 11,32,35,64,88
ODOM
  John 7
OLD COURT HOUSE 21
OLLIVER
  Francis 27,39,40,42,43,
    47,53,68,76,79,86,91,95
ONSLOW COUNTY 73,80,89
OUTLAW
  Captain 63,87,91,98
  George 27,49,79
  James 3,5,13,14,17,19,
    20,23,25,39,44,53,57,
    61,63,64,69,81,87,89,
    91,95
OUTLAWS BRIDGE 12,25,28,81
OUTLAWS SLEW 26
PADGET
  Jacob 10,19
  Joab 7,34,47

PANTHER SWAMP 25,27,28,47
PARISH
  Stephen 50
PARKER
  Amos 62,73,80
  Daniel 9,24,64
  Fereby 69
  John 22,30,38,41,70
  Jonathan 24,64
  Peter 24
  Richard 8
  Widow 99
PATTERSON
  James 96
  James,Mrs. 96
PEARSALL
  Edward 2,5,9,10,19,24,28,29,
    36,37,47,53,54,67,72,83,85
  James 2,4-7,9,12-14,19,24,28,
    29,31,36,57-60,76,90,94,96
  Jeremiah 10,16
PEARSE
  Archibald 50,61
  Micajah 13
  Naomi 13
  Ruth 13
  Snodon 45,50,60,62
  William 4,13,17
  William Alexander 13
  Zilpha 17
PENNINGTON
  Noel 26,94
  William 25
PHIPPS
  Deborah 96
  Thomas 26,95
  Thomas,Jr. 26
  William 26
PICKET
  Henry 8,41,72,80
  James 17,69-73,77,80,86,89,90
  James,Jr. 4,80
  Margaret 99
  Solomon 43,73,78,80,93
  Thomas 4,70,90
  William 17,20,70,80
  William,Sr. 76
  William,Jr. 76,81
PICKETS LANDING 89
PIPKIN
  Asher 86
  Jesse 60
  Lewis 4
PLATT
  Adam 29,55
  John 26

POLLOCK
  William 27
PORTER
  Alexander 7,10,96
POWELL
  Britton 25,38,96
  Douglas 44,76
  Hardy 33
  Starling 27
POWERS
  Samuel 51
PRESCUT
  Richard 70,92
PRICES FOR TAVERN KEEPERS 98
PUCKET
  J. 51
  Priam 91
QUIN
  Abner 18
  Caleb 18,41,43,72,93,96
  David 26,63
  George 26
  James 26,63
  Thomas 1,2,10,15,17,
    76,93,99
RATLIFF
  Samuel 66
RAWLINGS
  James 8
REED
  Andrew 78
REEDY BRANCH 27
REEVES
  Adam 4,54,64
  Hardy 9,27
  William 63
REGISTER
  Jesse 60
  Joseph 60,62
REVIS
  Hardy 39
REVOLUTIONARY WAR SOLDIER 34
RHODES
  Jacob 4,14
  John 75,88,93,95
  Joseph Thomas 2,5,6,14-16,
    20,21,23,30,31,37,42,44,
    47,53,54,57,58,64,66-69,
    73,80,81,86-88,90,91,95,
    96
  Samuel 8
RIGBY
  William 4,14,15,47,53,
    83,85
RIGLEY
  William 80

RIVENBARK
  Frederick 40
  John 56,78
  Simon 25,35,79
RIVERS [?]
  James 43
ROBERTS
  James 35,37,77
  Jesse 35,37
  Richard 25
ROCKFISH CREEK 16,20,25,33,35,
  39,47,68,79,80,81
ROGERS
  Abel 20
  James 19,20,24,62,71
  John 18,20,22,49,63,92
  John,Jr. 26,63
  Mark 27
  Micajah 26,75
  Samuel 4,15,47,53,87
  Solomon 26,75
  Stephen 16,19,22,23,33,
    40,62,71,72
  William 26
ROGERS LANDING 19,20,24,81
ROGERS SLEW 27
ROLLINS
  James 38,70
  Robert 31,38
ROOTY BRANCH 87,94
ROUSE
  Elizabeth Mary 9,10
  Martin 9,35,37,41
  Philip 1,6,9,10,37,41,44,
    55,61,97
ROUTLEDGE
  Colonel 19,28,67
  Easter 29
  Nicholas 10,21
  Sarah 54
  Thomas 1-3,5,7,9,10-19,
    21-24,28,30-43,45,47-55,
    58,59,63,65,67-69,71-75,
    78,80,83-85,88,89,91,93,
    94,99
  William 29
RUNCIE
  Adam 36,99
RYAN
  James 35
SALMON
  William 75
SAMPSON
  James 44
SAMPSON COUNTY 4,18,33,38

SANDERS
   Alexander 26
SANDLIN
   Nicholas 20,31,81
   Samuel 51
SAVAGE
   William 75
SEWELL
   Charles 25
SHARPLES
   William 40
SHEARS
   Mary 34
SHEHON
   Henry 25
SHELTON
   Thomas 19,25,81,88
SHEPPARD
   John B. 55,56
SHOALER
   Martha 93
   William 93
SHOLDER
   William 20
SHUFFIELD
   No first name 61
   Ephram 27,64
   Isom 17,19,64,69,73,97
   John 4,14,27,96
   Lincoln 59,73
SIMPLER
   William 27
SIMS
   Robert 13
SINGAR
   Solomon 27,49
SINGLETON
   Richard 26,56,92,94
SLAUGHTER
   John 38
   Robert 38
SLAVES 2,19,20,24-27,36,38,
   45,52,58,61,65,69,74,75,
   80,81,85-87,90,93-95,97
SLOAN
   David 4,22,32,35,36,56,
     61,83,85
   Edward 26,63
   Margaret 22
   Robert 11,22,56,61,70,
     89,93
SLOCUMB
   No first name 65
   John Charles 26,80
   Samuel 8,86

SMITH
   Benjamin 2,15
   Betsey 52
   Celia 52
   Elizabeth 39
   Frederick 4,19,24,25,46,81
   George 35,40,59,62,67
   George,Sr. 29,36
   George,Jr. 47,62
   Ivey 4,29,47,67,76,77
   Jacob 39,43
   Job 50
   John 31,32,51
   Joseph 4,15,19,54,56,61,
     67,95
   Mary 39
   William 39,52,62
SNELL
   Roger 33
   Stephen 27,29,56,61
SNIPES
   Benjamin 26
SORACTA 28,29,56,93,95
SOUTH CAROLINA 4
SOUTHERLAND
   Captain 34,42,57,63,64,66,
     90,98
   Daniel 9,30,44,47,53,55,57,
     66,72,83,86,96
   John 19,24,75,81
   John,Jr. 72
   Phill 19,20,47,56,86,88,
     89,91,93,96
   Robert 5,19,28,29,32,
     41-44,68,93
   William 4,10,13,20,30,35,
     52,53,57,72,91,96
SOWELL
   Charles 81
   Lewis 92
   Samuel 1,6,7,10,25,46,56,
     60,76,81,89
   Shadrick 1,65,68
SPEARS
   Mary 32
SPENCE
   Isaac 27
SPILLER
   James 61
STAFFORD
   Josiah 59
STALLINS (Stallings)
   Captain 3,10,12,34,42,46,
     57,63,64,84,91,98
   Mesheck 16,40,72,75,79,
     83,88,89

STALLINS (continued)
    Shadrack (Shadrick) 16,29,
        32,33,35,36,40,45,56,60,
        65,79,88
STANLEY
    Moses 70
STEVENS (Stephens)
    Alice 78
    Barnabas 44
    Charles 78
    Eulee 43
    Mildred 43,65,71,78
    Suckey 78
    William 27,40,43,45,56,
        65,78,96
STEWARTS CREEK 16,21,47,
    62,71,72
STOKES
    Arthur 2,4,9,10,14,15,
        36,37,41,44,47,55,56,
        61,77,92,97
    Henry 78
    William 2,20,22,29,56,61,96
STONE
    James 26
    William 27
STROUD
    Lutson 2,20
STUCKEY
    John 27,94
    Lewis 27,94
SULLIVEN (Sullivan,Sullivant)
    Agga 69
    Ann 69
    Archibald 69
    Caleb 26,63
    Elkanah 69
    John 8,26,29,82
    John,Sr. 63
    John,Jr. 8,63
    Michael 26,63,78,80
    Owen 26
    Widow 26
    William 8,26,51,63,72,
        82,84,90,92,94
SUMMERLIN
    Mrs. 39
SULLIVENS SLEW 26
SWINSON
    Absalom 25
    Auston 25
    Jesse 26,53,63,70,75,
        83,85,95
    John 26,63
    Rich'd 25
    Theophilus 19,25

TANNER
    Benjamin 56,61,66
    Samuel 35,60
TAX 3,16,21,22,24,25,31-34,
    37-39,45 47 49,51-53,56,57,
    59,61,63,64,66,68,73,75-77,
    79,83,84,89,90,91,92,94,95,
    97,99
TAYLOR
    Abe 69
    Aly 99
    Catherine (Katharin) 75,87,
        88,90
    Demsey 24,64
    Elisabeth 79,96
    Jacob 10,87
    James 1,63,89,93
    John Vol. 22,40
    Jonathan 2,17,32,51
    Prudance 69,99
    Thomas 6
    William 5,10,17,26-28,40,
        45,53,54,56,57,63,64,74,
        75,79,85-87,93,96
TEACHEY (Teachy)
    Captain 3,63,91,98
    Daniel 2,3,5,16,17,19,31,
        42,44,45,53,54,56,57,63,
        64,71,78,91,95,96
    Daniel,Jr. 16
    Jacob 89
    Timothy 4,96
TEGUE
    William 80
THALLY
    Andrew 2,6,10,36,47,53,66
THIGPEN
    Job 80
THOALER
    Moses 73
THOMAS
    Isaac 1,4,15
    Jonathan 26
    Lewis 5,6,17,26,28,41,43,
        46,74,82,83,96,97
    Thomas 13,15
THOMSON
    Elizabeth 23
    James 14
    John 70
    Stephen 14,33
    Thomas 15
    William 20,23,32
THUNDER SWAMP 28
TILLIS
    Temple 89

TILMAN
   Charles George 26
   John 66
   Stephen 51
TIMMONS
   No first name 27
TUCKER
   John 34,71
TURKEY 21
TWILLY
   Joseph 75
   Robert 4[?],41,43,56,67,
     76,78,83,89,96,97
TYLER
   Owen 26
UNDERHILL
   William 27
VICK
   Joseph 94
WADE
   John 27
   Joseph 10
WADKINS
   Van 36
WAINE COUNTY 54,63,64
WAITE
   Daniel 46
WALKER
   Amos 27
   David 64
   William 10
WALLACE
   Andrew 29,65,80
   James 30
   William 4,15
WALLER
   Captain 10,12
   Elijah 50
   John 10,41,66,72,83,89
   John,Jr. 93,95
   Nathan 20,36,37,43
   Nathaniel 10,43
WALLIS
   Andrew 8
WARD
   Charles 2,3,7,15-17,19,
     21-23,26,28,31,34,
     35-42,44,47,49,53,54,
     57,59-61,63-67,69,71,
     73,75,76,78,80,84,85,
     87,88,91,93,94,99
   Daniel 92
   James 7,10,26,70,89,93,
     94
   John 5,48,66

WARD (continued)
   John,Jr. 27
   Luke 70
   Luke,Sr. 5
   Luke,Jr. 5,27,52,53
   Philip 70,89
   Samuel 5,7-11,19,27-29,
     41,44,47,48,65,68,82,
     84,94
   Ward 22
   William 4,9,27,40
WARDS BRANCH 27
WARDS SLEW 26,28,48,82
WATKINS
   Lavin 4,8,15,27,53,68,72,
     75,79,82,94
WEEDENS
   John 60
WELCH
   Thomas 19,24,52
WELLS
   Frederick 16,44,56,60
   Jacob 12,16,43,55,61,77,96
   Jacob,Jr. 56,96
   Martin 96
   Nathaniel 59
   William 34,50,51,53,60,61,
     65,77,79,83
WEST
   Samuel 95
WESTBROOK
   Demsey 64,87
WESTON
   Ruben 63,72,75,79
   Rubin,Jr. 26
WETTS
   Joseph 24,25,67
WHALEY
   Francis 10,81
   James 61
WHITE
   James 27
   Mary 64,66
   Penelope 69
   Robert 46
WHITEHEAD
   Captain 10,34,42,45,55,57,
     58,64
   Elizabeth 23
   John 19,26,33,36,37,45,64,87
   Solomon 23,33
WHITE OAK 27
WHITFIELD
   Bryan 30,38,77,88
   Needham 70

WHITFIELD (continued)
   William 30,35,36,83,
     85,87,88
   William,Jr. 62
   William, Minor 62
   William,Sr. 62
WHITMAN
   John 20,39
WIGGINS
   Elijah 22
   Thomas 4,6,10,27,55
WILDER
   Joel 73,88
WILKINS
   Abraham 81
   William 1,60,78,87
WILKINSON
   Robert 5,26,70,86
   William 27
   William,Jr. 4
WILLIAMS
   Aaron 4,14,16,36,55,
     56,60,65,68
   Benjamin 66
   David 4,51,60,95
   David,Jr. 89,93
   Frederick 10,33,35,47,
     68,84-87,91,97
   Gus 9,10,25,38,41,43,67,96
   George,Jr. 39
   Jacob 3,19,26,81
   James 6,29,50
   James,Jr. 19,25,81
   James,Sr. 10,11
   Jeremiah 20,30
   Joel 31
   John 5,7,16,19,25,28,29,
     35-37,41,56,60,70,73,
     79-81,83,85,95,96
   John,Jr. 47
   John,Mrs. 95
   Joseph 20,22,25,35,60,68,
     75,77
   Joseph,Jr. 16,25,44,47,72
   Joseph,Sr. 16
   Laban 10
   Mary 11,12
   Nathan 88
   Richard 4,14,29,30,56,60,
     69,77,80,83
   Robert 4,10,11,19,55,69,
     72,83
   Robert,Jr. 26,36,96

WILLIAMS (continued)
   Robert,Sr. 26,69
   Samuel 10,11,26
   Sarah 99
   Silvia 45
   Stephens 10,16,25,30
   Theophilus 2,3,5,7,8,10,11,
     15,20,23,27,36,41,43,46,
     48,72,75,82-84,86,88,98
   William 11,12,71
WILLIFORD
   Elisha 86
WILLIS
   George 25,59
WILMINGTON 20,34,47,62,64,65,
   71,80,85,97
WILSON
   Alexander 83,89,94,96
   James 75
   Joseph 30,96
WINDERS
   Edward 26
   James 10,26,63,67,70,94
   John 26,45,63,70,96
   John,Jr. 26,54
   John,Sr. 83,89- Thomas 79
WINDERS FOOT PATH 26
WINFIELD
   Joseph 8
WOOD
   Peter 92
   Simon 35
WOODWARD
   Elisha 55
   John 53,55
   John,Sr. 69
WORLEY
   Loftis 10,35,39,67,68,70,
     72,84,93
WRIGHT
   David 96
   James 2,5,26,36,47,53,82,
     83,89,95,96
   James,Mrs. 96
   John 9,23,28,33,59,95
   John,Jr. 9
   Thomas 4,26,34,49,59,65,
     83,85
YOUNG
   Arthur Dobbs 44
   Peter 42
   Sampson 44

www.ingramcontent.com/pod-product-compliance
Lightning Source LLC
Chambersburg PA
CBHW072055290426
44110CB00014B/1693